SRI LANKA — THE RESPLENDENT ISLE

Endpapers: Indigo light streams down between the branches of
a huge *mara* tree, one of hundreds lining the thoroughfares of
Colombo. Despite a recent construction boom, the city is still
green and spacious.

Frontispiece: This huge reclining Bouddha once occupied the
cave temple at Mulkirigala, near Galle. The engraving is dated
1744. The image-house shown is actually fully enclosed — the
artist has "cut away" the front wall for clarity's sake.

Title page: A brass effigy of the god Skanda, on sale at a roadside stall near his principal shrine. Skanda, one of Sri Lanka's
tutelary deities, is revered by Buddhists and Hindus alike.

Contents page: Bullock cart homebound at sunset.
South Coast, near Matara

Typeset in Benguiat by Superskill, Singapore
Colour separation by Far East Offset, Kuala Lumpur
Printed by Tien Wah Press, Singapore

ISBN : 981-204-060-9

Times Editions Private Limited
1, New Industrial Road
Singapore 1953

SRI LANKA

THE RESPLENDENT ISLE

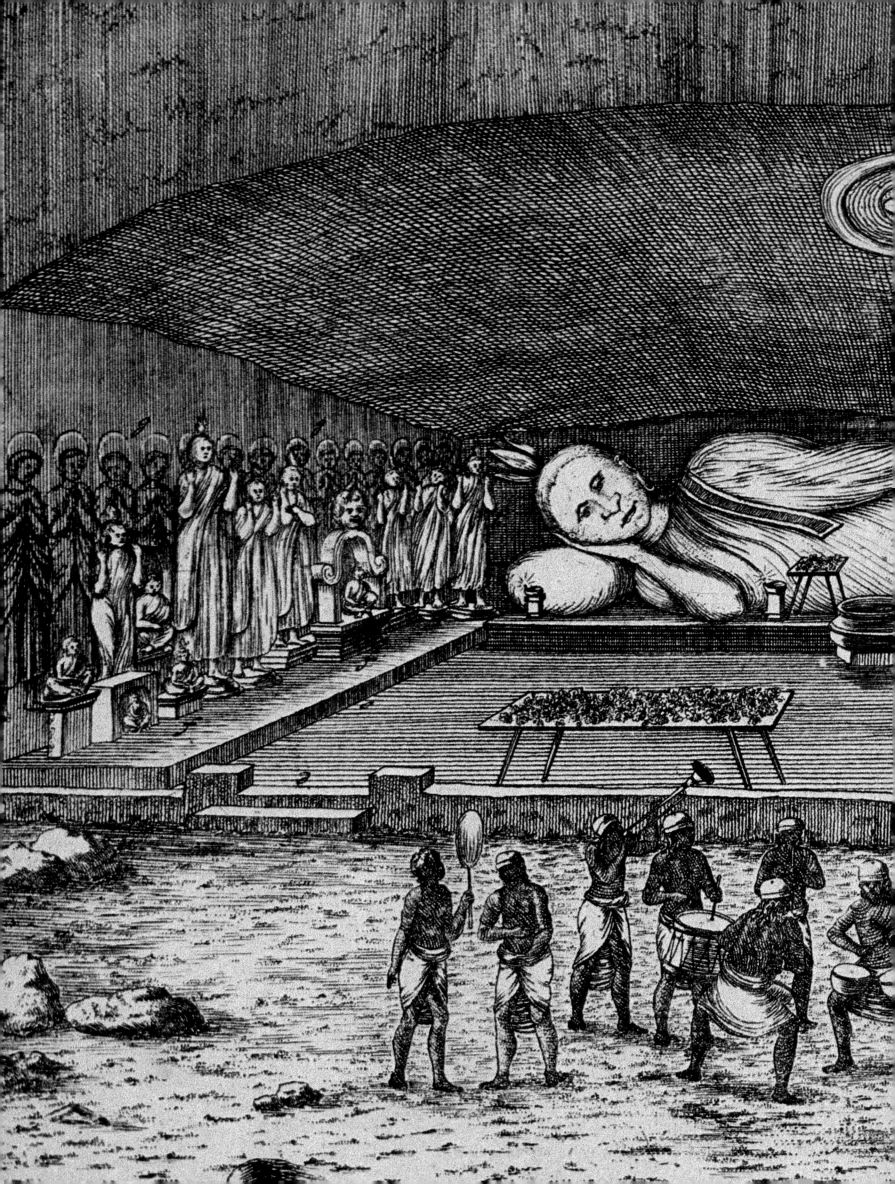

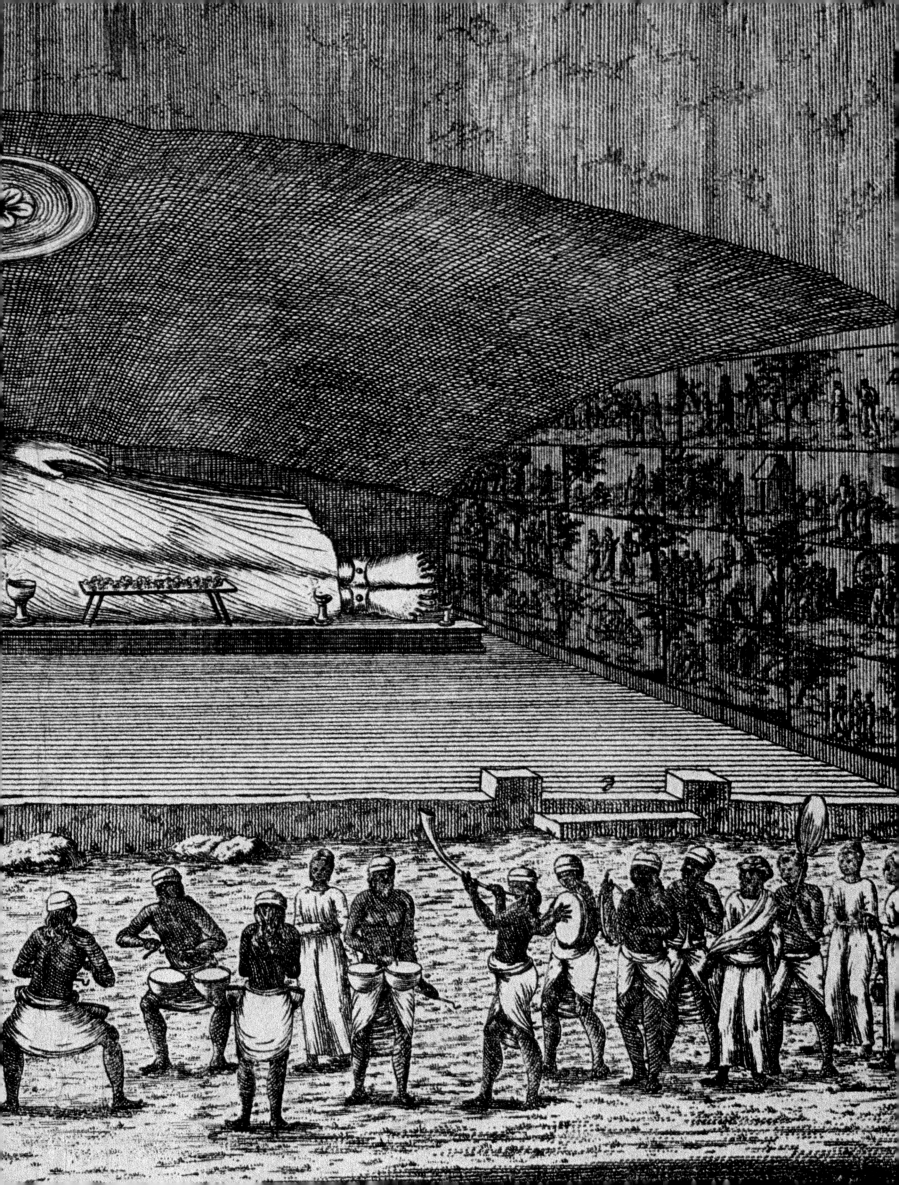

SRI LANKA

THE RESPLENDENT ISLE

Photographs by
DOMINIC SANSONI

Text by
RICHARD SIMON

TIMES EDITIONS

CONTENTS

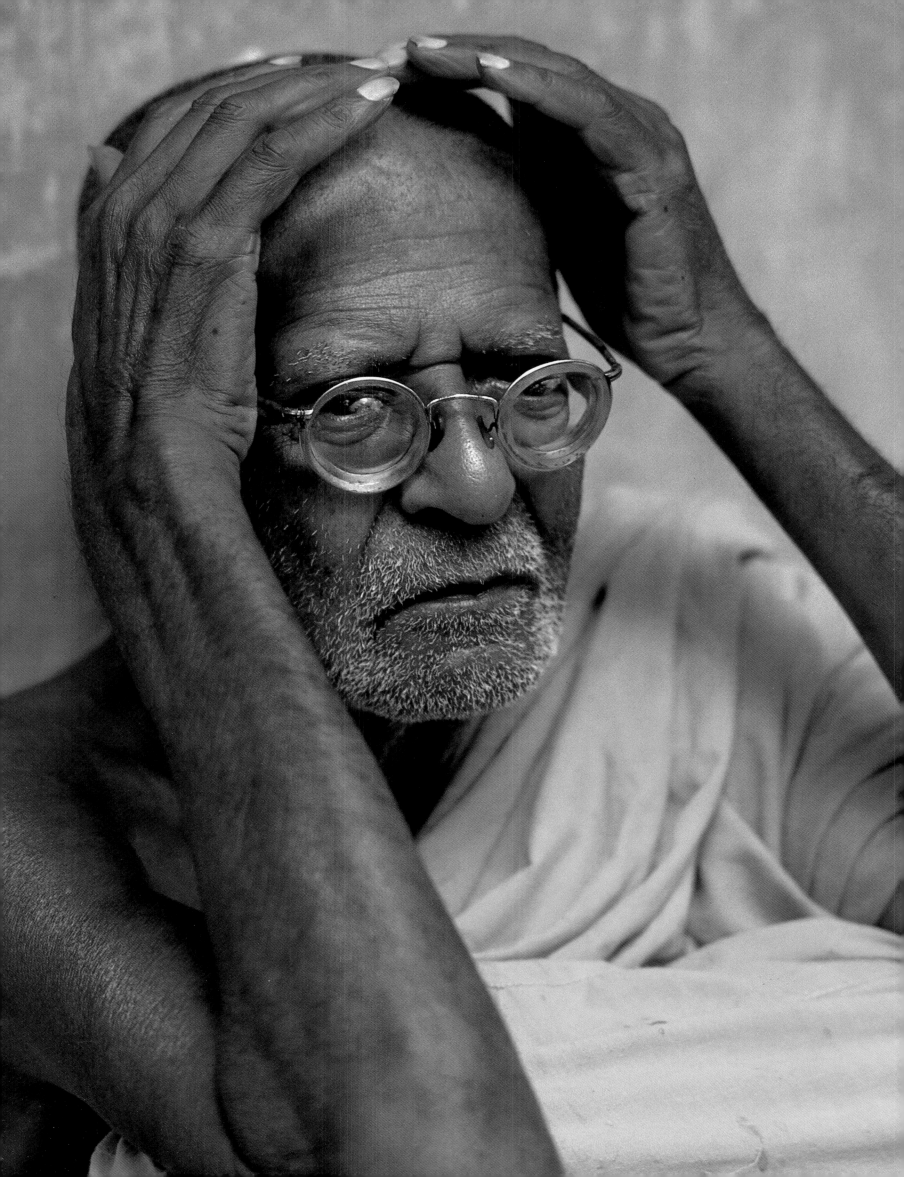

THE NATIVE PILOT

Notes for the journey

MY COUNTRY, SRI LANKA, REFUSES TO BE taken for granted. You can't ever sit back and relax, thinking you've got the measure of her, or she'll toss another surprise at you and make you realise you don't really know her at all. A couple of years ago, I set out to write an article about Roman Catholicism in Sri Lanka. I am not a Catholic myself, so this called for a good deal of research. The subject was well, if not impartially, documented, and I soon found myself

up to my neck in facts and opinions, not always sure which was which. I needed someone to help me sort myself out; some sources in Colombo recommended a certain erudite and fair-minded Catholic antiquarian, Father Anselm by name. And so one Saturday morning, I set out for Kalutara seminary, where the good father was to be found.

Colombo's urban sprawl has now spread well down the south coast, along the Galle Road as far as Kalutara. Even on a Saturday, there was enough traffic to make the journey a demanding one: Sri Lankans are not well-disciplined drivers. The chaos on the streets often terrifies first-time visitors, who cannot imagine how anyone can brave the tide of metal, the darting scooter-cabs, snarling motorbikes and crammed minibuses, and possibly emerge unscathed. That some of the slower-moving obstacles are undeniably picturesque — thatch-topped carts bumping along behind phlegmatic oxen, men rolling barrels of fresh coconut toddy, the occasional elephant — only makes matters worse. Yet once across the Kalu river and beyond the swarm of traffic and pedestrians around the Kalutara temple (where every Buddhist traveller must stop and make offering before journeying on), the congestion eased; and after turning off the main road a little farther on, we found ourselves driving along a pleasant rural highway, with paddy fields on one hand and gently rising, wooded hillside on the other.

I drove slowly, keeping an eye open for the turning to the seminary. But the great colonnaded gateway would have stopped me in my tracks even if I'd been doing a hundred miles an hour. There it stood by the side of the road, its plaster flaking and discoloured, a great Romanesque folly as out of place among the paddy-fields and scattered wattle-and-daub huts as an Aztec pyramid. A gravel driveway, weed-choked and rutted, ran under the central arch and disappeared among overhanging rubber trees a few yards up the hill.

It wasn't the seminary, of course. The latter was a mile or two further down the road, and by the time we reached it, the matters I had come to discuss reasserted their priority, and I forgot to ask Father Anselm about my roadside vision. But on the way back, with a brief glance at my companion, I swung the car off the road and drove through the great arch. I just had to know what lay at the end of that decrepit strip of gravel.

The westering light slanted through the ranked tree-trunks in thin, irregular shafts. The upward curve of the driveway soon blocked the main road from sight, yet the overhanging branches and the brow of the hill kept us from seeing our destination. Spotlit by the sun, a plaster statue glowed on a black plinth: a Greek goddess of the more discreetly-clad variety. Then the road steepened, and we found ourselves driving up a whole avenue of such statues — some intact, some missing a nose or an arm, others fallen from their pedestals and wrapped in creepers — towards an unseen hilltop *dénouement*. The architect of the place must have had a flair for the dramatic, for it was not until we crested the hill that the building which crowned it finally revealed itself: a vast and crumbling parody of an English manor house, set incongruously against a flagrant tropical sunset.

Out of the front door of this dream-palace poured a stream of small, half-naked boys. It was as if we had disturbed an anthill. They surrounded the car, pointing and chattering, until a young man clad in a sarong appeared, shooed them away and bid us welcome.

*Bikkhu, or Buddhist clergyman, Kandy (**left**). There are several chapters of the clergy, distinguished by the colour and drape of their robes and the other objects they carry. This layman (**above**) carries a smile under his handlebars.*

He seemed to take our arrival very much in his stride. He showed us around the house, pointing out only things that he himself liked: the rent and grimy portraits of Sinhalese grandees, the banqueting hall with its minstrels' gallery and ventilation ducts in the floor to blow cool air gently up dancing ladies' skirts. Everything was mouldy, cobwebbed and crumbling even though the building was plainly lived in. It turned out to be a boys' home. We never found out where the teachers and administrative staff had gone; there was only this caretaker, and his charges.

Yet from the few questions he was able to answer, and the old paintings and photographs hanging in the hall, we were able to piece together the story of the place. It was called Richmond Castle and had been built about the turn of the century by a certain Mudaliyar de Silva Wijesinghe, a wealthy Kandyan nobleman. Shortly after the building was completed, the old Mudaliyar died, and the property passed into the hands of his son. After a magnificent wedding at which the Colonial Governor officiated, the young master brought his bride home to Richmond. He fully expected to produce a long line of heirs, but that did not happen; instead, the couple remained childless. The palatial house, built for a dynasty, would have to fall vacant, or change hands after only one generation.

The thought would have galled a lesser man, but the younger de Silva Wijesinghe had inherited a full share of the romanticism which had caused his father to build a castle. Richmond would never hear the sound of his children's laughter; very well then, children not his own must be his heirs. Richmond Castle was willed into the Public Trustee's keeping, on the condition that it be maintained as a home for boys.

Public trustees are notoriously short of money, and the cost of the mansion's upkeep must have made it a ruinous inheritance. Yet the intention was honourable, and it is perhaps because of this that Richmond Castle retains its dignity in the face of the many insults its young occupants have submitted it to over the years. I like to think so, anyway.

I often tell the story of my Richmond Castle discovery, because it exemplifies the sort of unexpected delightful encounter Sri Lanka specialises in. This is the very birthplace of serendipity; the word itself derives from the name the long-ago Arab spice and gem traders gave the island: Serendip.

It is only this quality of serendipity that persuades me to write about my country at all. It is no accident that books of this sort are generally the work of foreign writers and photographers. The visitor has a sense of perspective ordinarily denied the native, who, being surrounded by trees, isn't too clear about the shape and extent of the wood. The visitor brings with him a whole set of cultural referents, useful for purposes of comparison. Accordingly, he perceives certain costumes, manners and ways of cooking salt fish as being highly exotic, therefore picturesque, and will endeavour to share those perceptions with the reader. If of an analytical bent, he may then go on to explain how all these things are not really so wonderful after all, but arise quite naturally from this or that aspect of the native culture. His readers will have no difficulty sharing his perception, for their set of referents will be the same as his. Neatly abstracted from chaotic, teeming reality, whole and self-consistent, *his* island becomes *their* island.

While researching this book, I came upon a set of photographs by Henri Cartier-Bresson which illustrates the situation perfectly. His Buddhist novices, Kandyan dancers and log-carrying elephants are common enough sights in Sri Lanka. Yet, when looking at the pictures, one sees the subjects from a new angle: the perspective of the photographer. Cartier-Bresson makes his subjects exotic, literally outlandish. One can well imagine stay-at-home Frenchmen looking over them and being struck by visions of an island Paradise. Shaven-headed boys in saffron robes! Log-carrying behemoths as wise as their mahouts! Bare-chested dancers swaying to the beat of drums before a mysterious domed and spired shrine! What must life be like among these wonders, far from the cold grimy rain-drenched streets and the rude, odiferous crush on the Metro?

It is just such a sense of wonder, of lives more meaningful or, at any rate, more colourful than one's own, that the writer or photographer strives after. Cartier-Bresson achieves it brilliantly — his black-and-white studies make most contemporary work look flat and tawdry. But could he have achieved anything like the same result if he had been a native of this country?

For the native writer or the native photographer, things are considerably different. Familiarity with his own land, his own people, has left him with a poor eye

*This painting (**right**) from a Buddhist temple depicts an episode from the Nimi-jataka, the stories of the previous reincarnations of the Buddha. Sesath, or ceremonial fans in the shapes of the sun and the moon, are marks of royalty; only kings walked underneath them.*

for the 'exotic'. Sunstruck beaches, drowsy wattle-and-daub villages, brooding primaeval forests are no new thing to him. He sees them everyday. Such sights can never be boring, but how shall he recapture the sense of wonder he felt on first encountering them, all those years ago? Remember, his island is composed of very different elements, of rush-hour traffic and local politics, the price of cigarettes and a remark someone made last night at the club. Immersion in the stream of events makes detached observation all but impossible. The passenger on the riverboat sees a broad, calm mass of water rolling with stately deliberation towards the sea. How can the river-pilot make him understand that other stream, the swirling, treacherous monster with its vortices, boils and sandbars, upon whose back the pilot rides?

Perhaps the analogy itself might throw up an answer or two. For the native writer is, in truth, a river-pilot, steering the vessel of his reader's imagination through waters unfamiliar to it. The hazards he must avoid are the camera-toting clichés and chamber-of-commerce boosterism that abound in guidebook country. Swamps of irrelevant detail, tributaries of purely domestic interest, sandbars of platitude, all must be steered carefully clear of. The trip up the river must be full of strangeness and glamour for the passenger, who never notices, as he watches the beautiful moon rise through the palm-tops that line the opposite bank, how the pilot has angled the boat to give him the best possible view. And when the voyage is over at last and the final page turned, the reader must have gained, not merely a sense of faraway places, colourful festivals, magic, mystery and mazy philosophy, but also a little sense of what it might be like to pass one's life among these things.

As I say, it is only Sri Lanka's serendipitous nature which makes us imagine we can achieve this. The continued surprises, daily encounters with the unexpected that the country affords her people, keep her nearly as fresh in their imaginations as in a visitor's. Is it any wonder that travellers down the ages have fallen in love with her, sung her praises in tones of delirium, and cast aside their sensible, mercantile lives to live forever in her bosom? Sri Lanka's history tells of countless discoverers who came upon her by accident, fell in lust or love according to their fashion, and stayed. They were not always kind to her, but they taught her much, and miraculously, they did not mar her beauty. If she is complex and mysterious today, it is partly their doing.

And complex she is indeed. Sri Lanka is no dreamy tropical Eden inhabited by happy primitives, with no past and a dubious future. She is ancient, unpredictable, almost supernaturally wise, and not at all easy to describe. This is especially true when one is trying to look at her from two perspectives at once, but that is what we must do: an ambitious trick, but the only one worth turning, for a pair of native pilots.

Sesath bearers, Kandy Perahera. Carrying these ceremonial fans, they will attend on dignitaries who walk in the procession. Visnu the Preserver (right) and Laksmi, goddess of prosperity, look down on the crowd at a kovil in Colombo.

The Seven Ages of Man look down on visitors to this South Coast temple. **Following double page**: "The Buddha with the Emerald Eyes" at Subhodrarama temple, Dehiwela. **Pages 18-19**: The reclining Buddha at Gal Vihare in Polonnaruwa is the centrepiece to what has been called "the finest sculptured group in the world."

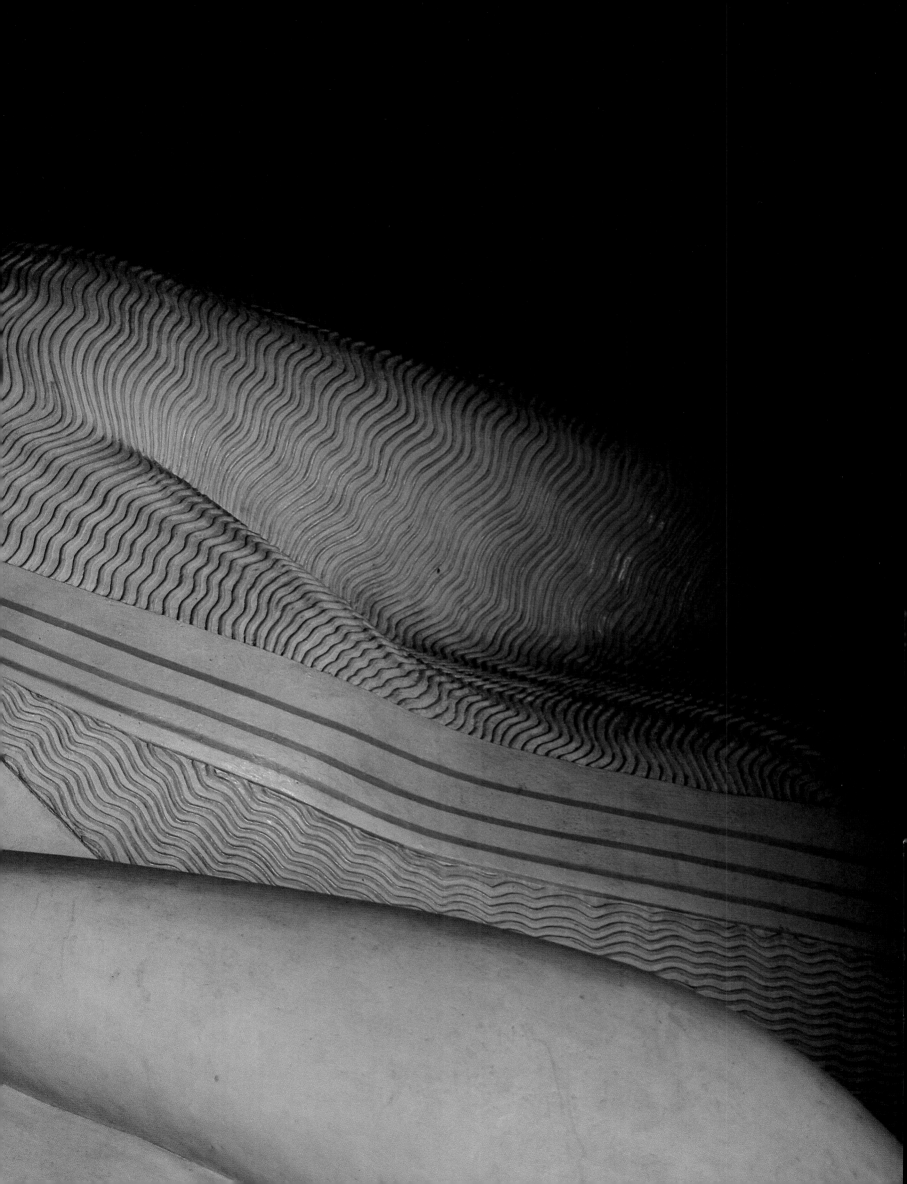

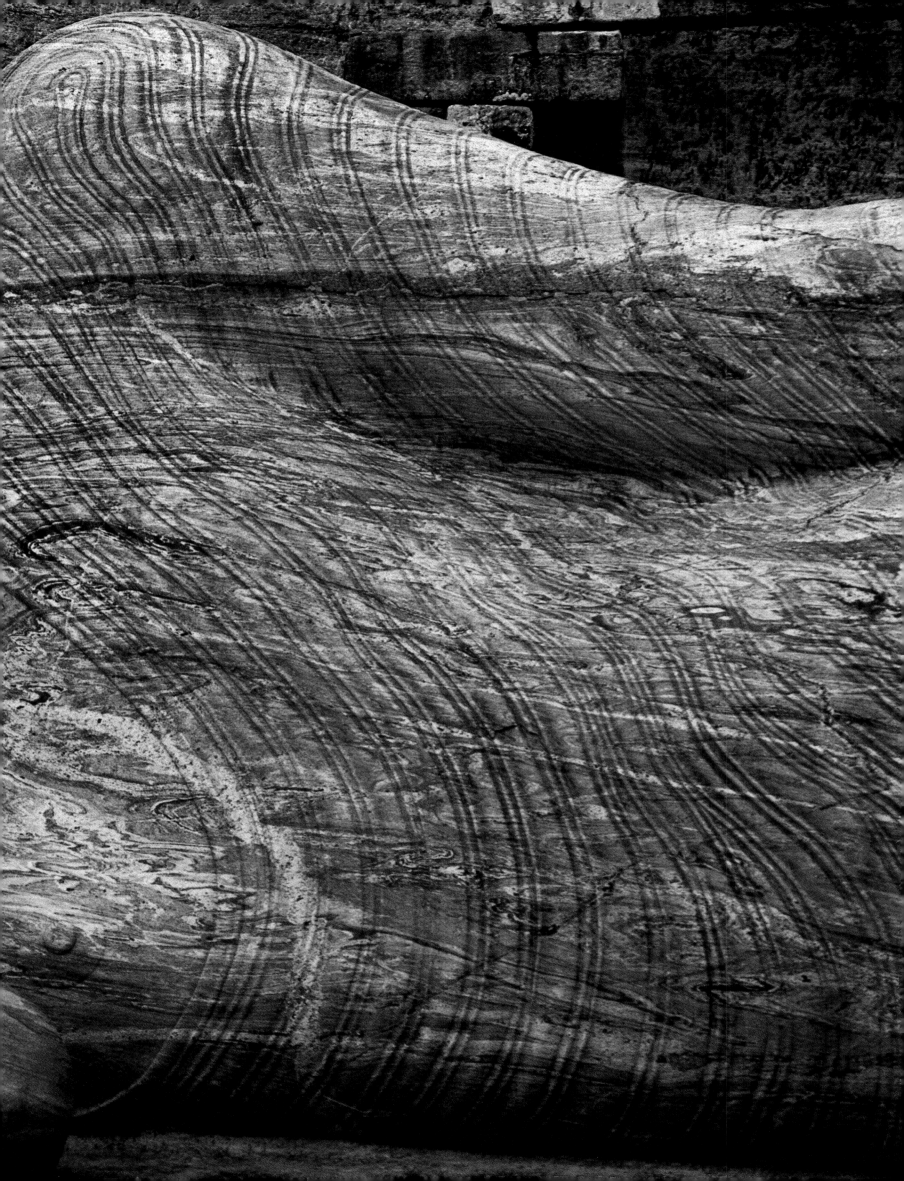

LANKA
Children of the lion

THE SIXTH CENTURY BC WAS ONE OF HIStory's golden moments. It was as if some god had touched the planet with genius. In Ancient Greece, Pythagoras and his followers were laying the foundations of western thought, while in India, a prince named Siddharta Gautama left home, family and worldly goods to seek, and find, enlightenment. Farther east, Chinese civilisation was in full flower, with Confucius and Lao-tzu setting forth their opposed

but strangely complementary philosophies. It was a time of great empires and cultures: Babylon, Persia, Greece. It saw the birth of Rome.

It is impossible to say exactly when, but one evening, during the dry season of a year somewhere near the middle of this century, a caravan was on its way from the capital of Vanga, in Bengal, to King Bimbisara's fabled city of Maghada. Aboard was a stowaway. Well, not a stowaway exactly. The young girl who had argued and cajoled and begged her way into the trader's company barely minutes before the caravan set off obtained her passage legitimately enough, in the end. But that was only because she was dressed and talked like any other urchin girl, and offered to make herself useful with the cooking and laundry. She looked as if she might be pretty, but under the rags and the grime, it was hard to say. Anyhow, her looks may have helped her case a little. But even if she had been as lovely as Helen, the honest traders would have had nothing to do with her, had they only known her true identity. Their new kitchen-maid was the King of Vanga's daughter.

Princesses can be famous for a variety of things: beauty, grace, wisdom, even cruelty. This one had a different claim. She had a reputation for wild and amorous ways, but that was not the reason why her parents kept her locked night and day inside the palace. Her incarceration was due to the prophecy that shadowed her life: one day, the soothsayers said, this princess of Vanga would become a lion's mistress.

If the caravan had reached Maghada, the story of Sri Lanka might have been different. But the princess, who had escaped from the palace in disguise to seek her fortune with the traders, had an appointment with fate. She kept it in the forest of Lala.

The lion seemed to appear out of nowhere, springing into the middle of the narrow forest path roaring like a wind from the heart of the sun. There were screams and cries of warning. Carts toppled. Sacks and bales fell and burst open. The company scattered in all directions. Princess and lion moved towards each other. The girl remembered the prophecy, and was not afraid; in fact, the emotion she found herself feeling was very different from fear. She assayed a tentative caress, and the lion was "roused to the fiercest passion" by her touch. Putting her on his back, he carried her away to his den, and there, the soothsayers' prophecy was fulfilled.

This story can be read in the *Mahavamsa*, the great chronicle of the Sinhalese people, who make up the majority of Sri Lanka's population. It is the story of that people's origins and is exactly as true as the tale of the she-wolf's sucklings, Romulus and Remus, the founders of Rome; that is to say, it is one of those myths on which a people's conception of itself is based. Biologists would tell us that the Vanga princess could not possibly have had two children by the lion. The *Mahavamsa* tells us that she did, children named Sinhabahu and Sinhasivali.

The boy, Sinhabahu, was as brave and strong as a lion's son ought to be; strong enough, by the time he was sixteen, to roll away from the den-mouth the huge rock with which the lion had imprisoned his human family. Freed by her son, the princess returned to the world of men, taking Sinhabahu and his sister with her. Later, Sinhabahu was to kill his father, without recognising him. Shortly after, the old king of Lala died, and the people crowned Sinhabahu in his place. The new king took his sister to wife, and they had sixteen pairs of twin sons, the oldest of whom was named Vijaya.

*Once thought to represent the disciple Ananda, this large standing figure at Gal Vihare (**lit**, "rock temple") (**left**) is now generally recognised to be the image of the Buddha himself. The blue-skinned saint Moggalana (**above**) was one of the Buddha's principal disciples. Detail from a Buddhist temple painting.*

The history of Sri Lanka really begins with Vijaya. The Lala prince inhabits a misty realm somewhere between history and legend. Did he truly exist, or is he only a symbol standing for the adventurous North Indian migrants who were the first to record their discovery of the island? Sri Lanka's history is full of such discoverers, and often it is through their eyes that we see her most clearly. Flesh or fable, Vijaya was the first of them. He is also the symbolic ancestor of the race whose name, in their own language, means "people of the lion's blood".

Prince Vijaya had the heroism which went with that blood. He also had more than a fair share of his mother's headstrong temperament. Although he was Sinhabahu's heir, his conduct, and that of his followers, grew so wild that the Lala people rejected him and demanded his execution. Fortunately for the unruly prince, his father decided that banishment would be a sufficient penalty. Vijaya and his men were shaven like convicts, forcibly embarked on ships, and cast out to sea. Their families went with them.

They ought to have perished, but serendipity, that principle of happy accidents, favoured them. And so it came to pass that, on the very same day the Buddha laid down his body and passed into nirvana, the exiles' fleet made landfall on a copper-coloured beach. King Vijaya of Lanka had arrived to claim his kingdom.

Concurrence with the Buddha's death would date Vijaya's landing exactly: May Full Moon, 483 BC. But no one knows if the sacred coincidence actually did take place. It does not really matter. Like most legends, this one serves a truth above mere facts, for it is impossible to tell the story of Sri Lanka without telling of the great religion that found its safest sanctuary here and shaped the ways of most of its rulers and people for the better part of 2,500 years.

But the story really begins long before that. According to the *Mahavamsa*, the Buddha himself visited Sri Lanka three times before Vijaya arrived, coming and going by miraculous ways. The chronicle claims he came to subdue and convert the *yakkhas* and *nagas*, rebellious demons or nature spirits who were the island's only inhabitants. The first visit ended with the banishment of the *yakkhas* to the hill country. The second, to end a war between two tribes of *nagas* over a gem-set throne, resulted in the object of contention being presented to the great sage by the warring parties. On his third visit, says the chronicle, the Buddha travelled throughout Lanka and left his footprint upon the sacred mountain, Adam's Peak.

Historians speculate that these *yakkhas* and *nagas* were mortal men, long present on Sri Lanka. The *Mahavamsa* disagrees, but the Chinese traveller Fa Hsien, writing a century before the author of that work, records that these 'spirit beings' carried out a lively trade with visiting merchants! Certainly, Sri Lanka had men living on it before Vijaya. In fact, *homo sapiens* may have arrived as long ago as 500,000 BC.

Aside from whatever conclusions can be drawn from relics of a Stone Age culture discovered in the Balangoda district, very little is known about these early inhabitants. Sri Lanka does feature in the famous Indian epic, the *Ramayana*, as the kingdom of Ravana, the evil monarch who steals the hero's bride: the hero, Rama, rescues her after a tremendous battle in which the gods play an active and partisan role. The *Ramayana* is often uncannily accurate about geographical detail, but its gods, heroes and villians act too fancifully for us to make anything but vague and general guesses about the culture and ways of prehistoric Sri Lanka's inhabitants from their doings.

So, although the story begins long before the coming of the prince and the passing away of the master, we know too little of it to tell. Afterwards there was a great deal. Fortunately for us, the tale was not only told, but written down.

*The stone Shivalingam, or phallus (**above**), is a symbol of the generative forces in nature. The hands echo the old alchemists' motto: "As above, so below." The superb gold Skanda figure is from the community kovil of the Nattu-Kottu-Chettiyar, a group of hereditary goldsmiths, near Galle.*

THE GOLDEN AGE
Of temples, reservoirs and dynasties

SRI LANKA HAS NEVER LACKED FOR VISITORS eager to tell their version of her story. For her own people's account, however, we must return to the *Mahavamsa*, and its sequel, the *Culavamsa*, which takes up the story where the former leaves off, around 300 AD. Written in ancient Pali by Buddhist monks who were, understandably, eager to show their country and religion in the best possible light, the *Mahavamsa* and *Culavamsa* are inevitably somewhat one-

sided. However, this does not diminish their value as guides to Sri Lanka's storied past. After all, how many history books can claim to be free from bias or exaggeration? Once this is understood, it is possible to accept the chronicles for what they are: a brilliant and poetic interweaving of fact and significant myth.

Eleven hundred years of their country's eventful history had already passed by the time the patient monks began inscribing the Great Chronicle onto leaves of *talpat* palm. They worked under the supervision of its author, their abbot: a royally-connected monk named Mahanama. The year was 500 AD or thereabouts, and King Moggalana I was sitting upon the throne of Lanka. The place was Anuradhapura.

Today, Anuradhapura is one of the world's largest archaeological excavations. In Mahanama's time, it was an elegant and populous capital city already 900 years old. It was also the centre of a flourishing Buddhist civilisation that covered the whole island and was then coming to the end of its first Golden Age.

Vijaya's dynasty lasted six hundred years. Anuradhapura, the capital from which his descendants and their successors governed, was founded by King Pandukabhaya early in the fourth century BC. Its name is popularly, and wrongly, translated as "City of Ninety Kings". Anuradhapura certainly saw a great many monarchs in its time, but the city is more likely to have been named after some dignitary called Anuradha, or, as some historians claim, after a constellation of that name which was in the ascendant when Pandukabhaya laid the first foundations of his capital-to-be.

Pandukabhaya's Anuradhapura was a planned city, and later monarchs were careful to follow his lead. There was little of the urban sprawl that bedevils

large cities today. The *Mahavamsa* describes ancient Anuradhapura's varied quarters, each occupied by people of a particular caste or occupation. Archaeological siftings confirm the description: a city of parks and water gardens, of tree-shaded boulevards and huge stupas shimmering like clouds brought to earth.

Anuradhapura lies at the centre of Sri Lanka's arid northern plain, and Pandukabhaya is credited with developing a system of reservoirs to supply the city with water. These early irrigation works were a forerunner of future wonders; over the centuries, the entire island would come to be covered with an intricate tracery of canals and reservoirs, in which great man-made lakes glowed like jewels. Necessity compelled these, for much of Sri Lanka is flat plain which receives little rainfall and retains less; yet the ancient Sinhalese triumphed so gloriously over necessity that Lanka soon came to be known as the Granary of the East.

But we are getting too much ahead of the story. Anuradhapura's Golden Age was still far in the future when King Devanampiya Tissa went hunting, and loosed his arrow at an elk-stag.

Like so many of the visitors who came after him, the Buddha conceived a special affection for the island of Lanka. As he lay between two *sala* trees, taking his leave of the world, the gods assembled to wish him farewell (for he was going to a place where not even the gods can follow). The dying master had a last request to make. He made it of Sakka, or Indra, as he is better known: would the King of the Gods take the island of Lanka into his special care? Sakka was glad to oblige, and placed the guardianship of Lanka in the hands of the god Visnu. Visnu thus became one of Sri Lanka's four tutelary deities: Natha, Visnu, Skanda and Pattini.

*Previous double page: Acrobatic dwarfs, called ganas, gambol around Kelaniya temple, near Colombo. This guardstone at Tiriyai (**left**) dates from the Polonnaruwa period; it represents nagas, half-human half-serpent spirits, portrayed as guardians of the Buddha. The lion detail (**above**) is from an Anuradhapura temple stone.*

The blue-skinned god set about his duties at once, appearing to Vijaya and his companions in the guise of a holy man, and pronouncing a blessing upon them.

Vijaya, however, was no Buddhist. Nor was his descendant, Devanampiya Tissa, on the morning of the day he set out from Anuradhapura, dressed for the hunt. Spiritual matters were probably very far from the King's mind that morning, although he may have thought a bit about the message he had lately received from Emperor Asoka in India. The Emperor wrote that he was sending his son (some accounts say brother), Mahinda, to Lanka to preach the Way of the Buddha to the people of the island. He did not add that Mahinda, like his master, had his own miraculous ways of coming and going, and by these means had already arrived atop the mountainous rock of Mihintale.

Mahinda could hardly be said to have "discovered" Sri Lanka; the surprise, on this occasion, was all on King Tissa's side. As the hunting-party approached Mihintale rock, it started a stag, which fled before the King's arrows toward the exact spot where Mahinda and his attendant monks stood waiting.

Mahinda identified the King first, and then himself to the King. The hunting-party, coming upon a group of robed men in the thick of the forest, was inclined to suspect witchcraft, so some explaining had to be done. Introductions completed, Mahinda then set to testing King Tissa's fitness to receive instruction in the dhamma by means of this famous riddle:

"What, O King, is the name of this tree?"
"It is a mango-tree, arahat Mahinda."
"Is there another such, besides this one?"
"There are many mango-trees."
"And trees other than those that bear mangos?"
"Of those, a great many also."
"And are there, besides the other mango-trees, and those trees which are not mangos, still other trees?"
"Indeed; there is this mango-tree."
"You are wise, O King!"

And so Devanampiya Tissa passed the test of the circular riddle, and Mahinda, along with his monks, returned with the royal hunting-party to Anuradhapura. Buddhism had come to Sri Lanka, almost two hundred and fifty years before the Christian era began.

Devanampiya Tissa ruled Lanka for forty years. During his reign, the Emperor Asoka died in India, and his great empire began to disintegrate. Soon the Hindu states of southern India, which were becoming more and more openly independent, began to look speculatively at the rich and beautiful island lying just twenty miles offshore. Lanka no longer enjoyed Emperor Asoka's protection, and by 205 BC, the throne of Anuradhapura and the lordship of the island were in the hands of Elara, King of the Cholas.

Over-enthusiastic modern Sinhalese nationalists would like to portray Elara as a tyrant. The *Mahavamsa* states clearly that he was nothing of the sort. In fact, his 44-year reign was marked by tolerance and an almost excessively scrupulous justice. But despite the fairness and clemency of his rule, the Sinhalese did not take kindly to Elara. He was, after all, a foreigner and usurper. The pre-eminence of Anuradhapura notwithstanding, the heartland of Sinhalese nationalism lies in the island's south, and it was from the south that a hero arose to challenge and defeat the Chola monarch.

Dutthagamini, or Dutugemunu, as he is more commonly known, was born in the southern kingdom of Rohana. His mother was a princess sacrificed to the sea by her father in atonement for a crime of clericide. Cast adrift upon a barge, she was rescued by the folk of Rohana, and became the wife of their king, Kavantissa. Dutthagamini, her eldest son, was destined for warlike deeds from his very conception; during her confinement, princess Vihara Maha Devi is said to have developed a craving for human blood. Nor would just any blood suffice; she would drink only the blood of a Chola warrior. Sinhala folklore holds that a pregnant woman's cravings are really the appetites of her unborn child. From the depths of his mother's womb, Dutugemunu was issuing a challenge.

It is not a pretty story; it probably started life as a piece of propaganda; but in the light of the obsessive fury with which young Dutugemunu conducted his campaign against the Cholas, it sounds appropriate enough. Like Alexander, Dutugemunu seemed born to war. Tall, strong, intelligent but prone to hotheadedness, the young prince soon became a master swordsman, archer and rider of warhorses and elephants. King Kavantissa, who preferred statecraft to battle, tried to restrain his impulsive son, but Dutugemunu refused to be deterred. He was going to end the Chola reign, and that was that. Sending his father a woman's ornament to shame him for his lack of resolution,

*The 12th century frescoes (**right**) on the walls of the Tivanka image-house in Polonnaruwa were painted using techniques similar to the much older paintings at Ajanta in India. Arranged in rows, as a series of sequential episodes, they depict scenes from the* jataka *tales.*

Dutugemunu took himself off to the hill country to plan his siege of Anuradhapura. Among the precipitous, central mountains, he assembled his army. As soon as news of his father's death reached him, he ran amok, spreading further confusion. It might have been simpler to sit back and starve the city into submission, but Dutugemunu could not afford to wait; reinforcements might arrive from India at any moment. He set his war-elephants to battering down the wrought-iron city gates. The boiling pitch deterred the beasts at first, but special armour added to several layers of buffalo-hide proved to be adequate protection, and soon the walls were breached. The Sinhalese host poured through.

Dutugemunu had private business with Elara. He challenged the Chola king to single combat, and the two met at the south gate. Both were mounted on elephants. Elara threw the first dart, and missed. Goaded on by his master, the Sinhalese champion's elephant impaled the Chola king's; at point-blank range, Dutugemunu hurled his dart, and Elara fell dead.

The battle was conducted with great chivalry and according to all the customs of single combat, but it was hardly a fair fight. After all, the Tamil king was an old man and Dutugemunu was in the pride of his youth. Yet the younger man hardly lacked in honour. He ordered a state funeral for his fallen enemy. Elara was cremated at the very place he fell, and a monument was built over the spot. Dutugemunu ordained that the site be venerated forever. Mahanama the chronicler tells us that the ordinance was respected by the kings of Lanka right up to his own time.

Dutugemunu had one more battle to fight. The reinforcements arrived, too late to save Elara, but not too late to be massacred. When the dust had settled, the Sinhalese once more ruled in Anuradhapura.

Like many retired warlords, Dutugemunu came to take pleasure in building. Even if his new enthusiasm had assumed the form of a series of monuments to himself, he might have been excused, others in his position having done no better. There are, or were, a great many Alexandrias. But there is no Gemunupura. Instead, Dutugemunu built for the church: temples, stupas and monasteries. Of his two greatest achievements, the fabulous nine-story chapter-house called the Brazen Palace and the enormous Ruwanweliseya stupa, only the latter remains. The former is no more than a poignant forest of stone pillars.

When the Ruwanweliseya was nearing completion, King Dutugemunu was stricken by the illness that was to end his life. Only the spire and a final coat of plaster were missing from the great stupa, but it looked as if the king might die before it was fully finished. Calling his brother, Tissa, to him, Dutugemunu ordered the younger man to complete the work.

Tissa loved his brother, so he prepared a humane deception. To mimic the look of plaster, he had a casing of white cloths made, and enveloped the stupa with it. A spire of bamboo scaffolding was added. When everything was ready, the king was brought in a litter to view the result. To his dimming eyes, the wood and fabric appeared as masonry and plaster, and King Dutugemunu died happy. The year was 137 BC.

The warlord from Rohana is the Sinhalese people's most adored hero. His memory has been besmirched in recent years through the attempts of modern chauvinists to claim him exclusively for themselves. However, driving out the Cholas was only his most picturesque exploit. The true test of his kingship came afterwards, when he set out to unite and pacify his fragmented kingdom.

The great dome of the Ruwanweliseya bears testimony to the wise and mature statesman who emerged, like a butterfly from its chrysalis, out of the fanatic boy. It is King Dutugemunu's finest, most enduring legacy to his people.

After his death, Dutugemunu's successors kept Lanka out of South Indian hands for thirty-five years. However Tamil power was to return again and again in the centuries to come, often staying for decades. Huge areas of the country came under their dominion from time to time, but these episodes always ended with the South Indians retreating across the Palk Strait.

The Jaffna peninsula, beach-head for most of these invasions because of its fine ports and proximity to India, has had a distinctly Tamil character since prehistory. Unfortunately, very little is known of the early story of the peninsula and its peoples. In the absence of a Tamil Great Chronicle in the vein of the *Mahavamsa*, scholars must scour legend and literature for whatever elements of the story these sources will yield. The archaeological evidence for a pre-Vijayan Tamil civilisation has not been firmly established; it is a subject which needs more study, but it is unlikely to get it until the current troubles are over.

Like "a flower fallen upon a rock", this lovely maiden floats hundreds of feet above the jungle, adorning the walls of Sigiriya.

The Jaffna peninsula was a prosperous region, whose character was quite different from the rest of the island. It contained, at Mantota in Mannar, Lanka's main port, harbour for Greeks, Persians and Romans as well as the Malabar seafarers who dominated the region's trade. The intercourse of cultures had made it sophisticated, cosmopolitan and wealthy. Mantota was "rich in gold, pearls and precious stones... peacocks danced in the cool shade."

In the South, the next great Sinhalese king was Dhatusena, who gained his throne as Dutugemunu had, by wresting it from the Cholas. In the tradition of the great kings who preceded him, he set about building vast irrigation works to transport the water on which his kingdom's life depended. His masterpiece was the Kalawewa, a vast artificial lake which holds 123.3 million cubic metres of water when filled to the brim by the Northeast Monsoon. During the building of the Kalawewa, an event occurred which foreshadowed Dhatusena's own violent death.

Work on the vast reservoir had been progressing smoothly enough, with the King himself frequently on hand to see how things went. No natural obstacle seemed too great for the royal engineers. But the hermit was a different matter. The old man had seated himself in the path of the advancing embankment and settled into a meditative trance. Neither the noise of construction nor the workmen's entreaties could stir him. In the end, the matter had to be taken to the king.

Sinhalese monarchs were not known for their evenness of temper. Dhatusena was no exception. Impatient of this impediment to the realisation of his most cherished dream, King Dhatusena thundered, "build the embankment over him!"

The King had two sons. Kassapa, the elder, was born of his first wife, a commoner. The second son, Moggalana, was the child of the Queen. A problem of succession arose. All might have been well if Dhatusena had not, in another fit of temper, put his sister to death. The sister's son, who was *senapati* (commander-in-chief) of Dhatusena's army, vowed revenge. Kassapa became his instrument. Befriending the prince, the *senapati* encouraged his regal ambitions and helped Kassapa win the people over. Moggalana, lacking support for what he saw as his rightful claim to the throne, fled to India. Dhatusena was imprisoned.

The *senapati* whispered to Kassapa that Dhatusena had hoarded up a treasure within the royal palace and was refusing to reveal its location. When pressed, the old king asked to be driven to the Kalawewa, and immersing himself in the waters, cried out, "This! This is my treasure!" Kassapa had inherited his father's temper; believing the *senapati*'s story, he had his father walled up in the Kalawewa embankment, leaving a slit in the old man's prison through which he could "gaze upon his treasure until he died". Justice of a sort had been served, although it is doubtful if the old hermit's spirit rested any easier as a result.

The ancient historians do not treat Kassapa well. In their view, he was not just a parricide, but a usurper. Worse still, he had committed the heinous crime of embracing a rival sect of Buddhism. Yet one cannot help feeling sympathy with Kassapa; he was a complex and mysterious man, with a strong philosophical bent. His life and reign were darkened by his crime, yet Lanka prospered under his rule and was at peace. And he left behind a monument that will endure, literally, until the mountains crumble. There is no need to mourn King Kassapa, for he is among the immortals. Sigiriya put him there.

Surrounded by flat forest plain, Sigiriya ("lion rock") rises 600 feet into the air, dominating the landscape for miles around. At the summit of this rock, Kassapa built a palace.

Sigiriya is a strange combination of monumental grandeur and aesthetic delicacy. The ramparts and moat that surround it, the monstrous statue of a lion that once guarded the path to the summit (and between whose forepaws the stairs to the royal pavilion ascended, so that to gain audience with the King one had to pass, as it were, through the lion's mouth), even the very conception of Sigiriya, the sky-palace hewn from granite: all these bear witness to a man who measured himself on a celestial, rather than a human, scale. Such a conception was perfectly in keeping with Kassapa's Mahayana Buddhist beliefs; according to these, a king was, in a sense, a god to his people.

But if Sigiriya were simply might made visible, it would be no more interesting than a score of other ruins. There is another aspect to the place, as there was to King Kassapa's complex personality. The parricide and usurper was a man of almost self-conscious refinement, an aesthete who had the sides of his fortress covered with mirror-finish plaster so that he might observe the northward passage of the clouds in them. That same sensitivity is reflected again and again throughout the design of Sigiriya, from the geometrically formal Pleasure Gardens at the foot to the intricately laid-out terraces at the summit.

Of all Sigiriya's beauties, the most celebrated are undoubtedly the frescoes of the Western Wall. Once the procession of lovely, bare-breasted women covered the entire face of the rock; today, only a score or so remain. Some were defaced by vandals in 1967, but these have been carefully restored, and the cloud-maidens are now as beautiful as ever.

It is said of beautiful women that they inspire poetry. This is certainly true of the frescoes. The remains of the Mirror Wall are covered in graffiti, scratched upon it by visitors to the fortress over the centuries following Kassapa's death. They are a far cry from the scrawls of contemporary vandals:

Dry as a flower/ That has fallen on a rock
Are the hearts of those beauties
Whose golden skin
Has caught my mind

Of the thousands of cloud maidens that covered the face of Sigiriya, only a few remain. To see them, one must walk along a narrow catwalk parallel to the rockface: underneath is empty space, and the jungle, hundreds of feet below.

The Ruwanweliseya Dagoba, Anuradhapura. King Dutugemunu's masterpiece, restored to its former glory, gleams behind a field of ruined pillars. Note the ganas, dwarf guardian figures, on the badly-eroded friezes around the pillar capitals.

One writer bemoans the ladies' silence:

We spoke / But they did not answer,
Those ladies of the mountain;
They did not give us
The twitch of an eyelid

Another answers consolingly:

She answers no-one
For her king has died

So he has. Kassapa's eighteen-year reign ended in 495 AD, as violently as his father's had. Moggalana returned, with his army of mercenaries. Kassapa descended from Sigiriya to meet him, and there was a great battle. Separated from his own troops and in danger of capture, Kassapa killed himself with his own weapon, carefully sheathing his knife after the fatal wounding. The reign of the god-king was over.

Recently, modern scholars have done much to refurbish the memory of King Kassapa. Senarat Paranavitana, doyen of Sri Lanka's historians, has pointed out that despite the massive fortifications, Sigiriya is far more than a redoubt built by a guilty and frightened king. If defence were its only purpose, a more utilitarian fort would have served much better. Sigiriya must have taken years to build, and eaten up a large part of the kingdom's resources.

Yet other theorists have claimed that Sigiriya's real function was mystical, or at any rate mystico-political. According to this school of thought, the rock-fortress represents Mount Meru, the cosmic mountain at the pivot of the entire universe where, according to Hindu (and therefore Buddhist) cosmology, the planes of existence intersect.

In this interpretation, each of Sigiriya's features has a transcendent meaning, and the ascent of the rock becomes a metaphor for the soul's ascent towards enlightenment, with King Kassapa, enthroned at the summit, representing the bodhisattva, the Buddha-in-becoming. Another of the Mirror Wall graffiti seems to support this theory: the author looks on the voluptuous painted maidens as representing the fleshly temptations he must overcome on his journey towards enlightenment:

Hail! / The one on his way to heaven is not
consoled by
The delicate doe-eyed ones
Standing here to
Captivate the sight by their splendour

Sigiriya: the Lion Rock standing almost exactly at the geometric centre of the island of Lanka. Whether as a last resort in time of invasion, or a focal-point for the strivings of the soul, the location is perfect. Perhaps King Kassapa was wiser than those who condemn him. Or perhaps he was, simply, wiser than he knew.

The end of the tenth century brought the curtain down on Anuradhapura. The ancient capital was set too far north to defend easily when the Cholas and their cousins, the Pandyas, attacked. Ever since the seventh century, the Sinhalese kings had retreated south-eastwards, to Polonnaruwa, whenever Anuradhapura became indefensible. In 993, the new city became the permanent capital. The City of Ninety Kings was abandoned at last, after more than 1,300 years. The new capital was itself scarcely established before it was overrun. In the early eleventh century, Lanka became a province of the Chola empire, with Polonnaruwa the seat of the colonial government. The Sinhalese went south again.

They returned in 1070, under the leadership of Vijayabahu I. After a siege which ended in a massacre, Polonnaruwa was back in Sinhalese hands, and the final period of Tamil dominion was over. Vijayabahu I was the liberator of Polonnaruwa. But it was another king who brought the city its greatest fame and glory: Parakramabahu I, called the Great.

Devanampiya Tissa was a great patron of Buddhism, Dutugemunu a warrior and architect. The god-king Kassapa was an aesthete, and a man of ambition. Parakramabahu was all these things, and a great many others besides. During his youth, the country was riven by political rivalries and wars of succession, and the unifying influence of the Buddhist priesthood, the *sangha*, negated by internal strife. Parakrama set about repairing these rents in church and state, using every means at his disposal: statecraft, family connections, espionage, the laws of hospitality and obligation. He soon came to be known as a man who applied highly questionable means to achieve unquestionably proper ends. By these methods, and by the more traditional course of armed confrontation, he united under his own rule a divided Lanka, and set to work to rebuild the ruined Polonnaruwa.

Parakrama re-erected the outer walls, then laid out streets, temples, stupas and public buildings within them. The result was a stunningly beautiful city, the plan of which ingeniously exploits the contours of the landscape it stands upon.

Parakrama's Polonnaruwa was Sinhalese civilisation's second and greater Golden Age. The King never lost sight of his primary object: the happiness and prosperity of his subjects. Every one of his actions displayed this concern. The army with which he subdued the warring kingdoms was made up of volunteers only; those with no taste for battle could work in the fields instead. Once he was settled on his throne, the King set about a heroic programme of engineering works. The jewel in the crown of his achievement was the Parakrama Samudra, or Sea of Parakrama, the gigantic reservoir which irrigates the land around Polonnaruwa.

Parakramabahu was also the only Sinhalese king whose ambitions extended beyond the shores of Lanka. An insult suffered by his ambassador to Burma resulted in the despatch of an expeditionary force to that country. The army landed and killed the Burmese king, replacing him with another suited to Parakrama's taste. The King also answered a Pandya request for aid against the Cholas with a fleet that "obscured the horizon"; since the Pandya kingdom lay between Lanka and the Chola lands, he reasoned that an alliance with it would create a buffer against Chola invasion.

The greatest of all Sinhalese kings died in 1186, after a reign of twenty-one years. He left behind a capital city of awesome beauty, studded with art and architecture that includes the Gal Vihare figures, hailed as "the greatest sculptured group in the world".

Polonnaruwa endured until the early 13th century, but its story after Parakramabahu I is one of decline, terminated by the catastrophic Kalingan invasion of 1215. Malaria appeared and made most of the central plain uninhabitable; the jungle returned to reclaim land where once, green rice-fields stretched to the horizon. The greatness of Ancient Lanka was at an end.

The Sinhalese moved south again. Kurunegala, Dambadeniya, and finally Kotte on the southwest coast became the new capitals of the Sinhalese.

And then one day, rumour arrived in Kotte of a race of strange-looking people encamped on the south coast. They ate stones and drank blood, were fair to look upon, and moved restlessly about all the time. Their musketry was said to be very fine indeed.

The stones were bread, the blood was wine. The Portuguese had arrived.

Painting from a Buddhist temple near Colombo, part of a frieze depicting the Nimi-jataka, the story of the Buddha in one of his previous incarnations.

SERENDIB
An island of dreams

FOR ALL THE *MAHAVAMSA* AND *CULAVAMSA* have to say to the contrary, Sri Lanka's history might as well have occurred in complete isolation from the rest of the world. True, there are exceptions: Parakramabahu I's Burmese adventure, for example, and the restoration of the Buddhist priesthood by monks from Thailand, not to mention the frequent rude interruptions from across the Palk Strait. But all these were affairs with definite internal conse-quences. As far as the monks of the Mahavihare were concerned, the greater world outside need not have existed. However, the outside world knew Lanka well enough.

Knew her, moreover, by a host of different names: Serendib, Tapro-bane, Ceilao, Ceylon. The green is-land off India's coast was famous, be-cause there were, in those times, only two routes along which commerce be-tween East and West could pass. One was the famous Silk Road; the other was the perilous sea-road across the Indian Ocean. Ceylon was a major staging-post along the latter route.

One of the earliest accounts of Sri Lanka by a European visitor was given by Onesicritos, a companion of Alexander the Great. He describes a country divided in two by a great river, one half settled and the other populated by elephants of colossal size. Onesicritos would have arrived about the time Anuradhapura was founded, a very early bird indeed. He was followed by other visitors from the west, and by the second century AD, Ptolemy was able to compile a map of the island that made up in scale for what it lacked in accuracy. The great geographer gave Ceylon about twenty times the area it actually possesses; on the same map, India looks puny by comparison! Historians take the size to reflect the country's importance to the traders of the Roman Empire. Roman coins found at Anuradhapura and Sigiriya seem to bear the theory out, but it is worth remembering that another of Ptolemy's sources may have been a Lankan embassy to the court of Claudius, a century earlier. Diplomats, throughout history, have been notoriously prone to exaggeration.

Other discoverers arrived from the east. One of them, the Chinese scholar Fa Hsien, has left behind a detailed picture of life in early fifth-century Anu-radhapura, where he lived and stud-ied for several years. A somewhat less amiable visitation occurred a thou-sand years later, in the 15th-century, when an expedition from China kid-napped the King of Gampola. Until this embarrassing incident, relations between the two countries were cor-dial, and Chinese traders were wel-come guests in the ports of Galle and Colombo. One of them even sent gifts to a local temple, thanking the resi-dent deity for protection extended to his sailors. The gift is commemorated by a stone inscribed in Chinese, Per-sian and Tamil, the languages of com-merce in the region at the time.

Other frequent visitors to Lanka in those times were the Arabs. While Europe endured the Middle Ages, the tree of Islamic culture was in full bloom, and soon the real-life counterparts of Sindbad the Sailor had come to dominate the eastern sea-lanes. Instead of giant serpents, rocs' eggs and the Old Man of the Sea, they encountered the scarcely less exotic lands and peoples of the East. Ceylon was a favourite landfall; compared to the deserts of Arabia, the is-land's lush southwest coast must indeed have seemed like Paradise. Many settled here, to become the ances-tors of today's "Moorish" community.

Along came the Renaissance, and Europe was, so to speak, back in business. Marco Polo passed through Ceylon on his famous journey. He was followed fifty years later by his fellow-countryman, the Papal legate Giovanni de Marignolli, whose pretty conceit ("from Seyllan... may be heard the Fountains of Paradise") has been quoted rather too often in recent years.

Greeks, Romans, Arabs, Chinese, modern Euro-peans: sailors of every seafaring nation have, at some time or another, enjoyed the shelter of Ceylon's har-bours and the benefits of trade with her hospitable

*Previous double page: Musical British bobbies form part of a perahera on the walls of a temple in Dehiwela, near Colombo. Other figures from the same temple include prosperous Sinhalese (**left**), wearing tortoiseshell combs and period clothing; note cross on chain. Harlequins are also part of the procession (**above**).*

people. It was not until 1505, however, that someone thought of cornering the market for themselves.

As with many crucial events in Sri Lanka's history, it happened by accident. The southwest monsoon is usually over by the end of October. However, sporadic rainstorms, some accompanied by high winds, can sometimes continue into the following month. It is bad weather to go chasing Arab pirates in, but that is what Dom Lourenço de Almeida did.

He never caught them. Not long after it left Cochin, the Portuguese fleet ran into frighteningly rough weather. Things looked bad. Dom Lourenço was for turning back, but aboard the flagship with him fared a Franciscan monk who was made of sterner stuff. Friar Vicente wanted to press on, and in the end, the admiral bowed to his persuasion. When the storm abated, the fleet found itself off the coast of Galle, and sailed into the port of Kolontota (soon to receive a new name: Colombo). The date was 16 November 1505. The first Portuguese expedition to Ceylon had arrived.

It landed in the midst of a political shambles. The kingdom of Kotte had collapsed, with no less than three separate factions squabbling over the remains. In the north, the independent Tamil kingdom of Jaffna retained its integrity, but that was all. The unity of classical times was only a memory. Soon the Portuguese were in control of Ceylon's coastal regions. They might well have been content with these, for control of the coasts meant domination of the ports and conse-

quently of the Ceylon trade, their main concern. However, they soon became embroiled in local politics, with bloody results.

Retreating before the guns of the Portuguese, Sinhalese power moved inland, eventually taking refuge in the mountainous country of the centre. The kingdom of Kandy was the last independent Sinhalese nation; the Portuguese never subdued it. In the low country, things were different.

Soon, a second conquest began: the *conquista espiritual*. As soon as the Portuguese were well established, Franciscan, Jesuit and Dominican monks started arriving on the island in growing numbers, and the churches began to spring up. The *conquista* made rapid progress. The Catholic monks preached in the vernacular, which helped a good deal. And that kind of advantage was needed, because the Iberians were up against some determined resistance. In one horrible episode, Portuguese missionaries converted hundreds of the inhabitants of the island of Mannar to Roman Catholicism. The converts were immediately massacred by the king of Jaffna, the brutal Segarajasekeran VII. In revenge, the Portuguese seized Mannar and attacked Jaffna itself. Segarajasekeran surrendered, agreeing to terms of tribute, and the Portuguese occupied Jaffna. Occupying garrisons are rarely known for genteel behaviour, but this time the rape and plunder were so extreme that it caused a public uprising. The year was 1560.

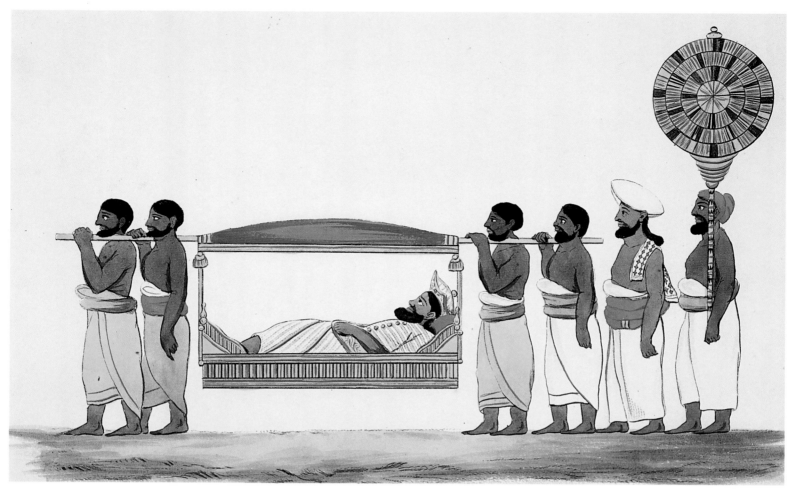

At least partly in response to such resistance, Portuguese suppression of Buddhism and especially of Hinduism, was thoroughgoing and ferocious. Here is an eyewitness account of the sacking of the magnificent Visnu Devale at Devundara in 1587:

"Thome de Sousa gave it over to the soldiers to do their work. They then proceeded to destroy the idols, of which there were more than a thousand of diverse shapes, some of wood, some of copper and several of them gilt. They then proceeded to overthrow the whole of the infernal machinery of the Pagoda, pulling down their domes and cloisters and breaking everything to pieces. They then sacked the store-rooms, in which they found a large quantity of ivory, fine cloth, copper, pepper, sandalwood, jewels and precious stones, and the ornaments of the Pagoda; everyone took what he liked best and the rest was thrown into the fire."

The Konneswar Kovil, or Hindu temple, at Trincomalee was pulled down to supply material with which to fortify the town. The "Temple of a Thousand Columns", as it was known, stood on a sacred site of prehistoric antiquity, a towering bluff overlooking the Bay of Bengal. In demolishing it, the Portuguese are said to have fulfilled an ancient prophecy.

Four hundred years is a long time indeed, and all the scars left by those grim events have long since healed. Pious Hindus continued to hold *pujas* at the site of the Konneswar Kovil, and today, a new kovil of much more modest dimensions, stands on Swami Rock. In it are images from the earlier temple, recovered from the seabed during the 1960s by the writer Arthur C Clarke and Mike Wilson.

Paradoxically, the Portuguese, despite the cruelty of their occupation, integrated themselves far more completely into the culture than the Dutch and British who succeeded them. The Roman Catholic church, for example, is well and truly established in Sri Lanka. Perhaps as many as one-fifth of the Tamils are Roman Catholics, and Jaffna is nearly as full of churches as it is of kovils. In fact, it is probably the most important legacy the Portuguese left behind.

It is certainly not the only one. From the thousands of Portuguese-derived words in Sinhalese speech to the equally numerous de Silvas, Pereiras and Fernandos who fill the telephone directory, the influence of the Iberians is visible everywhere.

A Dutch officer, looking about him as his company marched into the newly-occupied Fort of Colombo, observed that the Portuguese had built as if they meant to stay forever. Perhaps they did. Certainly, the people of Ceylon could not possibly have got rid of them unassisted. In the end, it took an alliance between Rajasinha II, King of Kandy, and the merchant princes of the VOC, the Dutch East India Company, to accomplish that. The bargain was that

Plates from the first English translation of the Yakkun Nattanawa, *or "Devil's Dance", published in 1829. They represent the* Yamma Raksaya *or Death Demon (**far left**) and the* Sooniyam Raksaya *or Demon of Darkness (**left**). The 1843 engraving (**above**) portrays a Kandyan nobleman in his* muncheel *or litter.*

This Dutch map of Ceylon is from a rare volume by Johann
Wolffgang Heydt, published in Wilhemsdorf in 1774. The Dutch,
unlike the Portuguese, mounted no major expeditions inland.
The land beyond the coasts was terra incognita.

The Dutch embassy of 1736, en route to treat with the kings of Kandy. Ambassador Daniel Aggreen, in his palanquin, is at centre, second row from the bottom.

the Dutch should recover the coastal regions of the island for the Sinhalese, in exchange for trading rights. In retrospect, it all sounds hopelessly naive. Naturally, the Dutch decided to keep the ports for themselves. Rajasinha, commenting on the deal he had done, remarked that he had exchanged "pepper for ginger" (a Sinhalese metaphor to signify a bad bargain). The reference to spices was appropriate, but it was really cinnamon the Dutch were after.

In the days before refrigeration, the preservative qualities of cinnamon made it enormously valuable. Until the late 18th century, Ceylon was the world's *only* producer of cinnamon, and the Dutch enjoyed a profitable monopoly. By judiciously manipulating the market, they managed to keep production constant for decades, while demand increased and prices spiralled upwards. Only de Beers, the diamond monopolists, have managed the same trick since.

The Dutch East India Company did very little with Ceylon except exploit the land as methodically as possible. Under its rule, Sinhalese culture suffered badly, not from suppression so much as from neglect. The Kandyans, who still held stubbornly out, came to see themselves as the last heroes of the Lion race and to look down on their subjugated low-country cousins. That view is still held by some of the more reactionary Kandyan families and remains part of modern Sri Lanka's tangled system of class and privilege.

Few contemporary Sri Lankans are able to trace their ancestry back to the Portuguese. The enormous number of Sinhalese with Portuguese names confuses the issue and besides, it all happened such a long time ago. With the Dutch, however, it is a very different story. The modern descendants of the East India Company's officers and men, as well as other Europeans, are the Burghers of Sri Lanka. Generally fair-skinned and English-speaking, the Burghers maintain a definite cultural identity, although in recent years their numbers have been sadly depleted by emigration. The 30,000 or so who remain are slowly being assimilated into mainstream Sinhalese culture, and soon they will be no more. Unlike Eurasian communities in other countries, the Burghers played a prominent role in the cultural life of independent Sri Lanka. Active in government, business and the arts, they served as interpreters of the cultural transition for the rest of the Sri Lankan middle-class.

The Dutch left little else behind. They were fine builders and lawmakers. Jaffna, in the north, is home to the Groote Kerk, or Great Church, and dozens of buildings give the north a strong Dutch architectural character. And the Dutch codified the traditional law systems of the Tamils and Sinhalese, forming the basis for modern Sri Lankan law. But by and large, the influence of the Dutch was almost completely eclipsed by those who came after them.

The third wave of European colonisation to break on the shores of Ceylon came from another island, as different from balmy Serendib as if it were another world altogether. The British took a long time getting here; they conquered the rest of the world first, and saved us for dessert.

In 1796, the Royal Navy seized the coastal ports of Ceylon from the Dutch. But unlike their predecessors, they did not stop there. The year 1747 had seen a weakened Kandyan kingdom pass by marriage into the hands of a South Indian dynasty, the Nayakkars. Even though these Hindu monarchs patronised a Buddhist revival, their grip on the kingdom was not strong enough. Encouraged by this, the British soldiers moved against Kandy. The first attack, in 1803, was repulsed, the natural citadel of the hill country proving impregnable once again. In the end, even the mighty British Empire needed a little help. Ironically, the Kandyans themselves supplied it. In 1815, internal divisions caused the kingdom to be ceded to the British, and Sri Vickrama Rajasinha, the last independent king of Lanka, was shipped off to India, a prisoner. The news is said to have so affected Sir Robert Brownrigg, the Governor, that he burst into tears at dinner and congratulated his guests.

A last convulsion, the "Great Rebellion" of 1817 to 1818, was ruthlessly put down. The colonial administrators who followed Brownrigg inherited control of a nation whose teeth had been well and truly pulled.

The British, in their time, did a great deal for the colony of Ceylon. Experienced empire-builders, they knew the value of good communications and proceeded to supply them: roads, railways, the telegraph. A proper civil administration was set up for the first time; the Dutch and Portuguese never really bothered. Although their mercantile rapacity was no different from that of their predecessors, the hard-eyed young agency men who came "out East" to seek their fortunes were at heart romantics, being British, and the *pax Britannica* was very real to them.

Fortunes were easy to find in those days. The Colebrooke-Cameron Commission, which proposed measures aimed at establishing a laissez-faire capitalist economy, made it easier. Soon, Ferguson's Ceylon Directory was listing firms with names like Carson, Cumberbatch & Co., Miller's, John Keells' and the like. The current edition still carries these names, though for the most part the ownership of these "agency houses" is now in Sri Lankan hands.

Ceylon's economy was founded on commercial agriculture. Coffee was introduced in the mid-1830s, and soon replaced cinnamon as the colony's major export. The great coffee blight of 1869 eventually wiped out most of the plantations, but fortunately a lucrative replacement crop was handy. In 1867, an enterprising Scot named James Taylor began growing tea at Loolecondera Estate, near Kandy. Soon the hills that had resisted foreign soldiers for so long were covered with a green carpet of tea, worked in the main by South Indian coolies who were imported in large numbers for this purpose, as well as to provide labour for civil construction. The British never mastered the trick of mobilising the Sinhalese to labour under them, and that is how the "lazy Sinhalese" rumour began, in spite of 2,000 years' worth of evidence to the contrary.

The mercantile economy created a new social structure. Money, not family, led to privileges. The old Sinhalese aristocracy, unused to the rough world of commerce, started to submerge. The new elite were mostly low-country Sinhalese, with some Tamils.

The British did a great deal for Ceylon; there was also much they did not do. Despite the new prosperity, the lot of the common people remained very much the same. The main difference was that now there was another sort of life with which to compare their own. Like most such comparisons, this one was invidious. The scenic beauty of rural Sri Lanka hid, and still conceals, a great deal of poverty and hardship.

The first rumblings of discontent were heard around the turn of the century, and took the unusual form of a temperance movement. Buddhism discourages the use of alcohol, which came to be seen as an evil foreign to the country. Soon other straws began to blow in the wind: the formation of a printers' union and the Ceylon Labour Party. In 1915, a fierce ethnic upheaval took place and was badly mishandled by the Crown. Still, things remained more or less in order, helped by the introduction of votes for all in 1931 (or nearly all: some of the populace still have no vote).

World War II arrived, and Ceylon threw itself completely and firmly behind Britain. On Easter Sunday, 1942, the same Japanese fleet that had earlier attacked Pearl Harbour launched a raid on Ceylon. With Singapore, the "impregnable fortress" laid low and Japanese troops advancing unchecked through Southeast Asia, the fall of Ceylon could have had fatal consequences for the Allies. Winston Churchill was later to say that he considered the Japanese attack "the most dangerous moment of the entire war". It passed without mishap, except for the deaths of a thousand Britons and Ceylonese.

In 1944, the war was practically won, and Don Stephen Senanayake, the Minister of Agriculture and Lands, submitted a draft constitution for an independent Ceylon. After some argument and emendation, it was accepted, and on 4 February 1948, the people of Lanka took charge of their destiny once more.

*Lions flank the side of this urinal stone, Western Monasteries, Anuradhapura (**left**). The splendid ornamentation was intended to show the monks' contempt for earthly adornment. The coat-of-arms of the Dutch East India Company, on the other side of the main portal at Galle Fort, bears an ironic resemblance.*

*The Thuparama Dagoba in Polonnaruwa (**above**) was restored by
Buddhist monks in 1848. This drawing was made by a European
visitor not long afterwards. This print of a Buddhist temple
on the West Coast, near Colombo (**bottom**), was executed
at about the same time.*

*This print of the Hermitage at Kurunegala (**above**) is by William Westall (1775-1850). The conical mountain in the background is Sri Pada, or Adam's Peak. Note the peacocks. The Water Carrier, by Samuel Daniel (1775-1811) (**below**) depicts the way water was supplied to the main cities of early 19th century Ceylon.*

A famous landmark of Colombo disappeared with the recent
demolition of Plate & Co's Galle Road premises. The studio was
specialised in portraiture, though the Burgher wedding study
(**above**) is by a rival photographer. **Following double page**:
A postcard of elephants bathing at Katugastota.

ROUND THE LAKE, KANDY, CEYLON.

MOHAMMEDAN MOSQUE, CINNAMON-GARDENS, COLOMBO, CEYLON.

SNAKE CHARMERS, CEYLON.

TAME ELEPHANTS BATHING, C

THE AWAKENING

The burden of freedom

INDEPENDENT CEYLON EMERGED INTO THE daylight blinking and rubbing her eyes. Although the train of events leading up to self-determination had been set going decades earlier, the actual event seemed to take the nation by surprise. After 440-odd years of colonial subjugation, Independence was going to take some getting used to. At first, there seemed little to it, anyway. The United National Party formed the first independent Ceylonese

government under Don Stephen Senanayake. The new Prime Minister made no major changes in the operating policies. Continuity, rather than change, was the watchword. His Cabinet of Ministers was made up for the most part of the same Oxford and Cambridge-educated parliamentarians who had run the country under the British. The Opposition was similarly composed. Except for a radical labour movement whose popular support was strictly limited to the urban areas, everyone seemed well pleased to maintain the *status quo.*

At the same time, it must have looked like the wisest course. Ceylon had substantial foreign reserves, mostly monies owed to her by Britain. As a Dominion, she remained within that country's sphere of influence and had a claim on British protection if ever she needed it. Education and medical treatment were readily available to all, and food, in particular rice, was heavily subsidised. The future glowed with promise; the promise of a parliamentary democracy after the British model, orderly and prosperous, governed by those whose education and social position perfectly suited them to the task.

But things hardly ever go as planned. Under the placid surface, other currents were at work. In the rural regions, the lives of the people did not change much. It always had a feudal character, which even the post-1931 ritual of casting one's vote had done little to alter. Independence had transformed the villagers into free citizens, but a real understanding of this freedom and of the rights and duties that go with it, would be slow in coming. Meanwhile, any number of opportunistic people would be only too eager to show them how to use the power that went with their newfound freedom. Special interests, chauvinists and just plain racketeers

vied with each other for a slice of the newly-baked political pie.

The Indian Summer of colonial Ceylon, which had lingered four years beyond its appointed time, came to an abrupt end when D.S Senanayake was thrown from his horse on Galle Face Green and died of his injuries. In that tragic moment, or rather in the intrigues and back-stabbing that followed it, the nation came to lose its innocence. The era of Parliament as a gentlemen's club was over. Not that the membership changed; nothing so radical. But from that time on, the behaviour and claims of the members would be increasingly dictated by voices coming from outside the smoking-room. Sadly, the true voice of the people was often the smallest, and least attended to. Far more strident were the voices which claimed to speak for them, but in truth spoke only for themselves. Preferment, corruption and communalism became the bugbears of Ceylonese politics. They remain so to this day.

The years that followed the death of Ceylon's first prime minister brought about many changes. Dudley Senanayake, old Don Stephen's son, succeeded him in office, but was forced to resign after a reduction in the rice subsidy created widespread unrest. He was to have another turn in office later on. Another Prime Minister, S W R D Bandaranaike, was assassinated by a Buddhist monk in an act of personal vengeance. There was a half-baked attempt at a military coup, an experiment in back-to-basics socialism, a Marxist insurrection. But all failed.

In 1972, the Dominion of Ceylon became the Republic of Sri Lanka. The change of name had different meanings for different people, but at least one of its implications was clear to all: from now on, we were well and truly on our own. Ironically, the

Previous double page: Mal lella (**lit.** "flower wood") fancy fretwork
*gives a wedding cake appearance to this manor house. A cloudy
poya day brings devotees and their offerings to Kelaniya temple
(**left**). The wearing of white is one of the austerities of sil, a period
meant for meditation. A temple figure faces outward (**above**).*

burden of freedom proved too much for the government that had declared it so boldly. At the end of its term of office, the country was almost bankrupt, and the 1977 election was a rout.

While the political roundabout went on turning, the apparatus of nationhood got erected somehow. Economic growth became the concern of government after government. Commercial agriculture was seen to be an unreliable money-spinner, too dependent on nature and fluctuations in the world market. Thus various measures were taken to stimulate industry, encourage foreign investment and diversify exports beyond the traditional tea-rubber-coconut orbit. The tea plantations were nationalised in the land reforms of 1972. Productivity fell drastically at first, but it picked up thereafter. It was well that it did; for, in spite of many attempts at diversification, a good year for Sri Lanka, economically speaking, is still a year when the price of tea rises at the auctions.

Meanwhile, the other agricultural sectors had to be rejuvenated. Bringing the Sri Lankan farmer into the 20th century has been an arduous process, but a rewarding one. New technologies and methods of cultivation have substantially increased rice and vegetable yields at harvest-time, but there is still a long way to go, with irrigation and fertilizer, before the paddy-farmer can make his acre as fruitful as, say, his Japanese counterpart's.

On the education front, there was change and change about. Sri Lankans are proud of their high rate of literacy, and education has always been a priority item during election campaigns and on the policy-makers' lists. The national university grew and offered a wider range of subjects for study, with campuses springing up all over the island. Public welfare also improved in such areas as health and housing, though it was not always fast enough to keep pace with the nation's and people's needs.

Large-scale development projects continued apace, often funded by aid from overseas. Western wallets opened more readily after the present government, which favours free enterprise and foreign investment, took office. One result has been a new attempt to realise a long-cherished national dream.

The Mahaveli is the greatest of Sri Lanka's rivers. Rising high in the central hills, it drains a substantial

A blue afternoon sky forms a backdrop for an assembly of saints atop the facade of St. Lucia's Cathedral, Kotehena, Colombo.

61

portion of the island's Dry Zone in its serpentine course before emptying into the sea at Trincomalee. It is not an easy river to live with, being unpredictable in both drought and flood. Worst of all, in a land where water is so scarce that people once husbanded it as the greatest of treasures, the river is (or rather was) a tragically wasted natural resource.

But the Mahaveli no longer flows unhindered to the sea. The once-wasted resource is being put to good use, the intractable brown god has been tamed and schooled to serve man. It will be some years before the Accelerated Mahaveli Project is finished, but the nation is reaping many of its fruits already.

The Accelerated Mahaveli Project is an ambitious plan to divert the turbulent waters of the river for use in agriculture and power generation. Crucial to it are several large dams, including two erected in the 1960s, that cross the Mahaveli along its 331-kilometre length. The largest of these dams, at Randenigala, fronts a reservoir that holds 860 million cubic metres of water when filled to capacity. The power generated by turbines at the Mahaveli dams had doubled the hydroelectric contribution to the national grid by 1987; that already large contribution will be increased soon. Meanwhile, down-stream, the resulting irrigation opens up new lands for rice cultivation, and settlers are moving in. The Mahaveli Project is one reason why, in Sri Lanka, unlike elsewhere in the world, migration from the villages to the cities does not pose a serious problem. In fact, It is the opposite that is happening: movement from towns to villages is frequent, helped along by state assistance and land grants.

At the same time, the environmental impact of the Mahaveli Project is not being ignored. Nature reserves have been established within the Project area, and recently a translocation of wild elephants took place. All the same, there are bound to be unforeseen ecological effects; after all, the Project implies nothing less than the complete ecological transformation of a quarter of the island's area.

Sri Lanka's population of 15 million people is awaiting that transformation eagerly. The Mahaveli Project promises them fertile and well-irrigated land, energy and prosperity in abundance. The attempt to tame the great river is their bravest venture since Independence. Its character recalls the hydraulic civilisations of Ancient Lanka, when enormous water-works made the land bloom and farmers prospered on land that only the jungle occupies now. And in the parallel with the ancient achievements, perhaps, lies the real secret of the Project's importance.

The people of Sri Lanka have always stood in the long shadows of those who preceded them. Our ancestors sometimes seem like giants to us; what can we, living amid the flotsam of colonialism, trying to synthesize a new culture at the uncomfortable confluence of East and West, show to compare with what our forefathers achieved?

The question nags at us, demanding an answer. When the Accelerated Mahaveli Project, and the 30-year master plan of which it is only the first phase, are completed, it will have one.

The port of Kolontota was already eight centuries old when Dom Lourenço de Almeida's Portuguese men-of-war dropped anchor there in 1505. The centre of Sinhalese power had long since shifted from the Dry Zone to the wetter, more fertile lands of the southwest, and the kingdom was now ruled from Kotte, a few miles inland from Kolontota. But while Kotte was the administrative capital, the coastal city was no minor suburb: over the centuries, a rich and bustling trading-port had sprung up here. Sinhalese, Malabars, Arabs, Persians and Chinese jostled each other in the crowded streets, and the druggy scent of spices drenched the warm, humid air; the city literally breathed the aroma of commerce. Hibiscus and frangipani bloomed in the gardens of palatial houses built with the spoils of trade. The rest of the country might know little of money, but here the clink of coins was a familiar sound.

Much, including the city's name, has changed since those times of early colonisation, but the picture is still the same in its essentials. Only the fragrance of spices is missing from the air of modern Colombo. It has been replaced by the smell of petrol-fumes. Otherwise, the city is still the same busy mercantile centre it always was, curiously unsophisticated despite its wordly materialism, and startlingly green and spacious. By day, it is hot, clamorous and dusty; night brings quiet and the coolness of the sea-breeze. Then the soothing sound of the ocean can sometimes be heard a mile inland, or more.

The fulcrum of the city is the old Lighthouse Clock Tower that stands at the junction of Chatham Street and Janadhipati Mawatha (President's Avenue) in the Fort. It is a strange location for a lighthouse, being a hundred metres or more from the sea, yet from 1857 until the 1950s, it served that function quite adequately. It was less successful as a clock, its massive escapement not even installed until 1914, and then rarely, if ever, keeping the correct time.

The clock tower stands right in the middle of an area known as the Fort. However, no ancient fortifications are visible here; these were pulled down a long time ago, after the British captured Colombo from the Dutch. Instead of keeps and dungeons, the Fort displays high-rise buildings and bank vaults. It is the city's business and financial district.

Other evidences of colonialism remain. In Cinnamon Gardens, the magnates' palaces still stand, looking like miniature English stately homes. In the upper reaches of the country's administrative and mercantile sectors, the customary lifestyle is modelled on that of the *sahibs*. There are cricket and rugby clubs, and even more exclusive clubs dedicated to the pursuit of tennis, rowing, swimming and golf.

*Closed doors keep the secrets of a temple outside Kandy (**left**). This image-house (**above**) in Panadura shows typical British-period ornamentation. Note fretwork eaves, or mal lella.*

These activities are conducted in an atmosphere of cane chairs, tea on the lawn and cocktails after seven. In April, when the heat becomes unbearable, everyone flees to the old British hill station of Nuwara Eliya to play golf, fish for trout in the artificially-stocked streams and drive fast cars into tea-bushes.

Colombo is a bustling city of one million souls, but at this level it is still a town where everyone knows everybody else. Strangely enough, the gossip network extends far beyond the orbit of the rich and powerful. Perhaps the still-strong influence of extended family ties has something to do with it, for the large expatriate community (British and other Europeans, Indians, Chinese) seems to be relatively immune to this local phenomenon. Whatever the reason, it is notoriously impossible to keep a secret in this city.

Farther down the social pyramid is where the real Colombo begins — the crowded, colourful, teeming life of an Eastern port city. Like all of its counterparts, it is a study in contrasts between rich and poor, high and low, past and future. Even the components of a traffic jam will display incredible variety: flashy sports cars, forty-year-old jalopies, bullock-carts and push-carts, container trucks, impossibly crammed buses, rickshaws, dozens of bicycles ridden by wobbling but imperturbable office clerks.

Colombo's mercantile flavour remains undiluted from mahogany-panelled boardroom to pavement hawker's stall. It is strongest in the Pettah, a compact bazaar just outside the Fort, where every saleable item on earth seems to have its own street of overflowing stalls or shops, and cash loans amounting to millions of rupees can be obtained at astronomical rates of interest (often payable by the hour) from penurious-looking men in dingy one-room offices.

Colombo was the capital of all Ceylon from 1815, when Kandy fell, until 1982, when the National State Assembly was moved from the old Parliament building in the Fort to impressive new quarters at Sri Jayawardhanapura in Kotte. The situation is now exactly as it was in 1505: Colombo is the mercantile and cultural centre, Kotte the administrative capital.

It will take time before the new seat of government attains the status of a true city. By and large, it is still very much a suburb of Colombo. The new Parliament building, set on an artificial island in the middle of a small lake, is a beautiful blending of

Lighthouse on the South Rampart of Galle Fort, near Utrecht Battery. The remains of Dutch fortifications can be found all along the south coast and in Jaffna. They are often in surprisingly good repair.

66

Dipaduttarama Vihare (**above**) in Kotahena, Colombo, is quite
uncharacteristic of Sri Lankan Buddhist architecture; it might
have been more at home in Bangkok. The Jumma mosque (**left**)
at Second Cross Street, Pettah. The building shows strong
Anglo-Indian architectural influence.

traditional motifs and materials with contemporary function; designed by Sri Lankan Geoffrey Bawa, it is not monumental in the Western sense, although it is a large and costly building.

One by one, the lesser departments of state are moving to Kotte, but most of them are still sited in Colombo, with the result that there is a heavy flow of traffic down the broad new highway that connects the two cities. Sri Jayawardhanapura (the name, incidentally, is traditional, and not connected with that of Sri Lanka's first executive President) also boasts a superb modern hospital, the best-equipped in the country. The residential suburb of Nawala, halfway between the new capital and Colombo, is growing rapidly as the latter's residential districts grow more crowded. Other housing developments are also opening up in the area. It may take years, even decades, but it looks as if the ancient royal capital of Kotte will once again recover its former glory.

Forty years have passed since the first day of Independence, but not nearly as many since Sri Lanka entered the modern world. That dramatic debut only really happened about a decade ago.

The various forces that have kept the nation and her people sheltered from the full impact of global culture are really too numerous and complex to examine in detail here. But in a surprising variety of ways, traditional patterns were sustained.

All this changed dramatically when the economy opened up at the end of the 1970s. The old colonialists used to say that trade followed the flag, which was an obvious lie, since anyone could see it was really the other way round. And so it was again in 1977. All at once, the island was open to trade with the western world; and all of a sudden, there was western culture right on our doorstep. It came pouring over us in a flood: television, magazines, hair shows and beauty pageants, consumer products from shampoo to styling mousse, supermarkets, caviar and cosmetics, marketing, motorcycles, *Mork and Mindy*. Conspicuous by their absence were Shakespeare, Descartes and Freud, but fortunately, they had already made it here, a few decades earlier.

Of course, this is a huge oversimplification of the matter, for it ignores the many centuries of contact with the West which Sri Lanka enjoyed (or suffered) before that time. But never before had the confrontation of cultures been so immediate or so all-pervasive. Sri Lanka became like a man who has dined rather too quickly and enthusiastically, off a large and varied menu; it all tasted very nice, but there is now a slight problem of indigestion.

Odd, incongruous little tidbits keep cropping up: the old lady whose tumour is being treated simultaneously by radiography, traditional *ayurveda* herbal medicine and a Christian faith healer; the tractor being extracted from the mud by a team of yoked buffaloes; the rich bachelor merchant with a carrot-juice-extractor capable of catering for a whole restaurant, proudly displayed in his apartment.

Images like these are not new in Sri Lanka; in fact, they are fast becoming a Third World cliché. But there are other images too, and these are not so charming. For the most part, the Sri Lankan people's "window on the world" is a shop-window.

For those who can afford what they see in it, this is all very well, but for those who cannot (and they form the majority), the picture often gives rise to frustration and resentment. Many of the nation's current problems can be traced, in the end, to this source. Unfortunately, there seem to be no easy solutions.

There are many who regret the suddenness of Sri Lanka's "coming out". Not all of them are sentimentalists or chauvinists; some are genuinely and intelligently concerned with the impact of western, or perhaps more to the point, commercial, culture on our own way of life. However, the time for debate is past, since the impact is already being felt.

The concerned ones can take comfort in the thought that cultures, too, change with the times, and strong, healthy cultures do so without losing their essential identity. The meeting of worlds was bound to occur, sooner or later; we had had a grace period of thirty years to prepare ourselves and centuries of experience to draw on in the preparation. Only time will tell if it was enough.

Except for some extremists (who are fortunately quite few), no one seriously wants to shut the window on the West again. Modern Sri Lanka has her injustices and inequalities, but retreating from the community of nations into an artificial shell of "traditional values" is not the way to cure them. The nation that gazed, newborn and sleepy-eyed, at the world of 1948 is wide-awake now, and eager to meet its destiny.

*The imposing facade of St. James' Church (**right**) at Mutwal, a predominantly Christian suburb just north of Colombo city.*

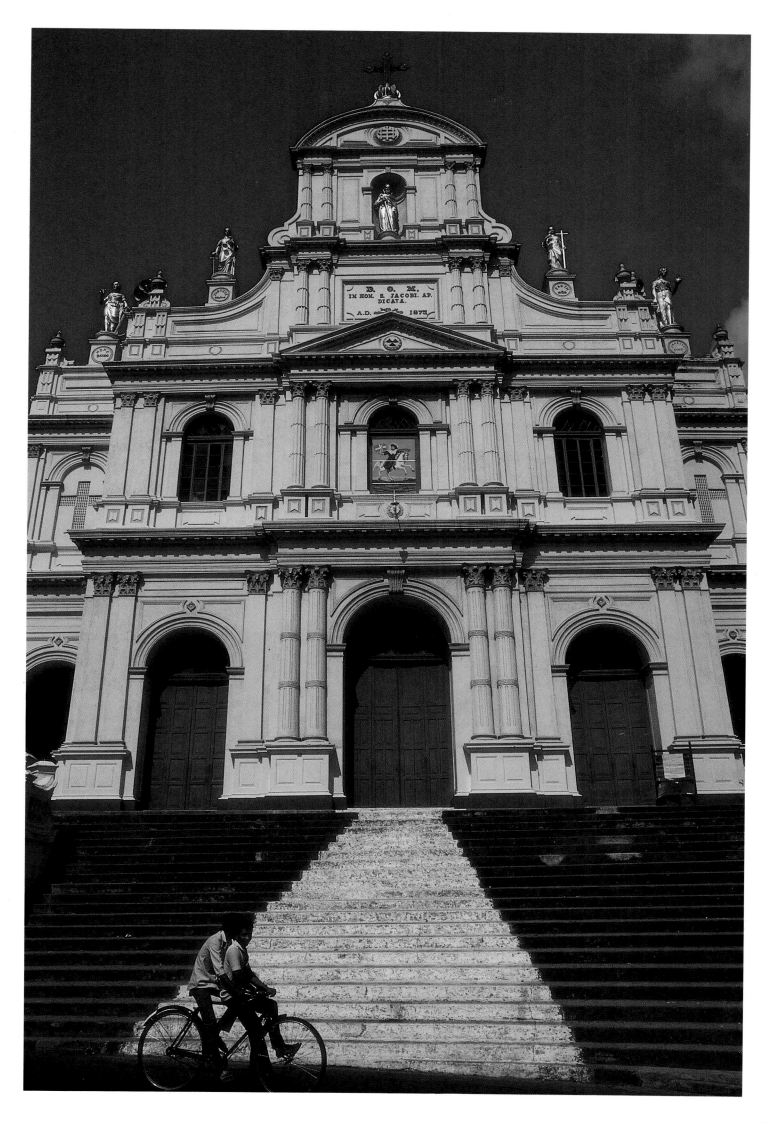

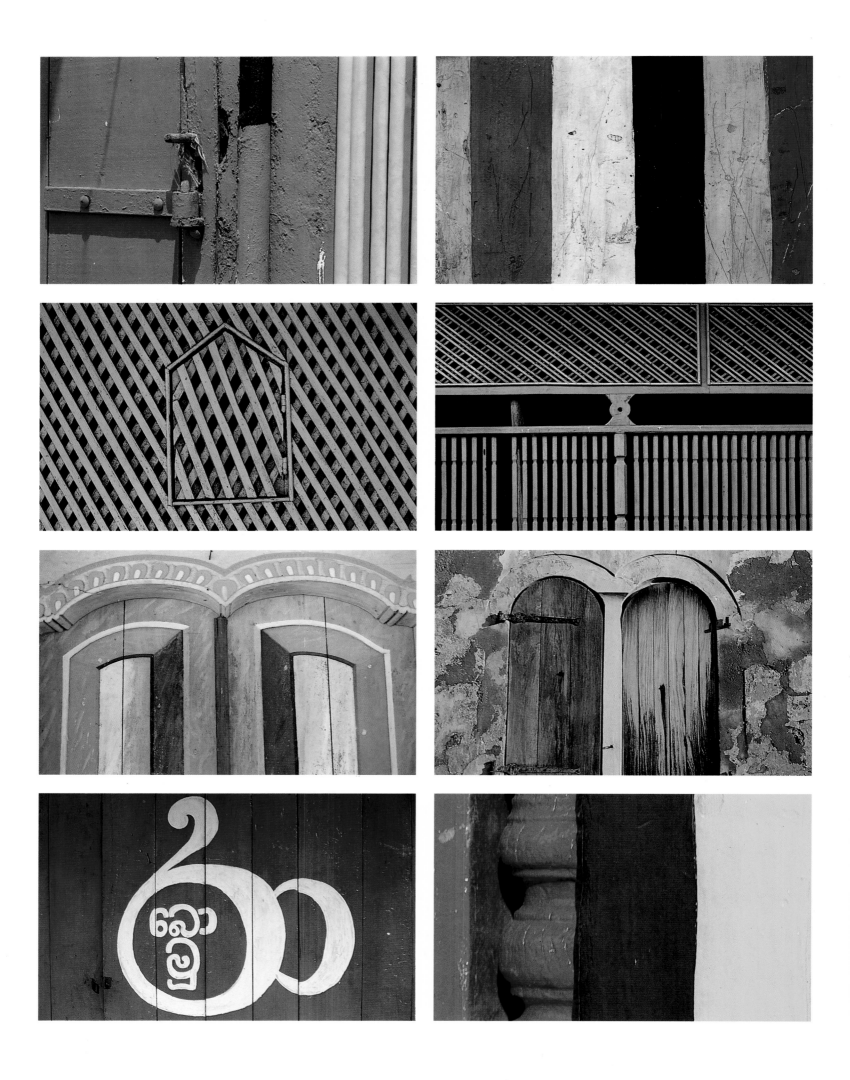

From left to right and from top to bottom: Shopfront and wall of kovil, Pettah; trellis Kurunegala; verandah, Colombo; door of a Buddhist temple; windows in Galle Fort; a country sight; kovil detail. Welcome to the East: barbershop door (**above top**). Sacred texts on the wall of a West Coast Buddhist temple (**above bottom**).

Studies in blue: houses and churches in the old residential district of Colombo and on the West Coast. Note the "mysterious East" window, the extensive mal lella decoration round the doors of No. 146, and the fanlight of the Dutch Post Office. **Following double page:** *The brightly-painted facade of No. 31, Messenger Street.*

SINHARAJA
The royal banquet

IT LIES SIX DEGREES ABOVE THE EQUATOR, A small island shaped like a pearl, a mango-fruit or, if you prefer more fanciful comparisons, a teardrop rolling off the cheek of India. It is a very concentrated teardrop, as though all the richness of Eurasia had drained into it down the long funnel of the Indian subcontinent. Sri Lanka contains more variety within its 65,000 square-kilometre extent than most countries three times its size. From Point Pedro in the north

to Dondra Head in the south, the island spans just four degrees of latitude, a mere 435 km. From east to west at its widest point, the distance is only 225 km. Yet within these confines are verdant plains sown with paddy, brooding tropical rain-forest, scrub jungle, marshland, dune and near-desert, mountain grassland, rolling tea-covered hills and soaring mountains wreathed in cloud. Around its periphery are some of the world's finest beaches. Despite Sri Lanka's small size, there are parts of it which are still unexplored.

Twenty-two rivers rise in the hill country and radiate outward to the sea. The land they drain was once part of the Deccan peninsula, the southern half of the Indian subcontinent. From time to time, Sri Lanka has been connected to this peninsula by a land bridge. Geologists tell us that the last time this happened was at least 10,000 years ago, but the great Indian epic, the *Ramayana*, mentions the bridge quite unambiguously. (The *Ramayana* was written a few centuries BC. Folk memory is a prodigious thing.) Airmen say you can still trace the contours of the bridge from the colouring of the ocean.

The seas around Sri Lanka are warm and shallow, with a definite continental shelf. This shelf, plus the coral reef that surrounds half the coastline, keeps sharks away; there are no recorded fatalities. On and around the reef swarms an almost scandalous abundance of life, moving in an endless, gaudily-costumed dance that is really a grim battle for survival. No one wins this battle, except the hoary old grouper who sometimes live for centuries. In the deeper waters off the continental shelf, where the big fish are, you can come upon practically anything: porpoise, whale shark forty feet long, actual whales. The variousness of Sri

Lanka is shared by the ocean that surrounds her shores.

The influence of that ocean keeps the island's temperatures fairly constant throughout the year. In the low country, these range from 23° to 30° Celcius, and in the hills from 11° to 23°. The southwestern region is hot and wet; the highlands cool and wet; the rest of the country hot and dry. Two monsoons bring rain every year. Each is named for the quarter from which it blows and the portion of the country it waters. The central hills divide the regions by obstructing the winds, and so prevent the entire country from being swept by the monsoons twice a year.

Although the Mahaveli irrigation project is rapidly opening up new lands for settlement, about half the country is still wilderness. In many cases, the jungle has returned to cover areas that were settled, irrigated and cultivated centuries ago, during the time of the great classical agricultural civilisations.

Not all the jungle is of recent formation. Covering the high mountain slopes and in isolated patches lower down, stand the last remnants of the primaeval rain-forest that once conquered the entire Wet Zone. The best-known of these is the Sinharaja, the Lion King's Forest, first-growth wilderness so old that it is almost unbelievable. Sri Lanka has suffered no major geological catastrophes to disturb its ecology, no earthquakes, volcanic eruptions or submerging land-masses. As a result, the Sinharaja has remained more or less unchanged for 100 million years.

It is a priceless natural heirloom, yet human incursions have caused its extent to dwindle to a mere sixteen square miles. Once destroyed, first-growth forest can never be replaced, for its life depends on the interaction of so many different species of plant and

*Previous double page: Anuradhapura sunset with the dagoba of Ruwanweliseya and coconut palms. A new road has stolen traffic away from the old seaside route (**left**) to Negombo, leaving it to bullockcarts and the occasional Transport Board bus. The long sleep of Anuradhapura (**above**) began in the 9th century.*

animal: a symbiosis that takes eons to establish itself, and is far too complex to be reproduced artificially. Every tree, shrub and vine, every bird and butterfly and beetle, every ant, grub and lichen has its own special task to perform in the maintenance of that mysterious life, the life of the forest, which includes them all and yet is more than they. Now this dark and lovely creature, the island's oldest inhabitant, is in danger of being murdered for firewood.

The Sinharaja has some very active champions, and educated Sri Lankans are generally conservation-minded, so there is hope. The danger is that such matters as the preservation of the forest are often ignored because of "practical constraints". That is to say, they cost money, or worse still, deny somebody the opportunity of making money. On a small scale, the battle of Sinharaja mirrors the plight of Nature every-where on earth. If she loses the battle, so shall we.

The Sinharaja is unique, but one can stumble upon magical experiences in any of Sri Lanka's forests, where, as in the deep ocean, anything might happen.

The diversity of environments this island offers is reflected in the profusion of plant and animal life it supports. Biologists, of course, have been aware of this ever since Carl Linnaeus, the father of scientific botany, published the *Flora Zeylanica* in 1747. Modern botanists have discovered and catalogued hundreds of Sri Lankan plants the great Swede missed; the count presently stands at over 3,000 different species. Living off this abundance of flora is the equally various animal life of Sri Lanka.

Imagine Africa, with its endless grasslands supporting vast herds of game, or a steaming Ama-zonian jungle where death dogs every footstep and the very air is thick with menace. Sri Lanka is not like that. Much of her wilderness is scrub jungle, difficult to traverse, but not impenetrable. Access has been made possible by the elephants, who have threaded the forest with their pathways; where an elephant has gone, a man can surely follow. Along these paths, the citizens of the forest reveal themselves in a series of casual encounters. Step as quietly as you like into a clearing, and the herd of spotted deer grazing there will still take flight; come upon the ruins of an ancient reservoir or tank, and watch the parade of the beasts which have come down to drink: wild boar, water buf-falo, sambhur (a pony-sized deer often erroneously referred to as elk), monkeys, barking deer, a host of others. Turn a corner on a jungle track, and come face to face with a leopard, sunning himself in the middle of the road. Instead of wide-screen spectacles, the jungle specialises in close-ups. Nihal Fernando, the country's premier wildlife photographer, writes of one of Sri Lanka's forty-odd sanctuaries that "(Wilpattu pro-vides) visitors with their thrills, not all at once, as in Serengeti or Tsavo, but in a series of surprises."

In the 12th century AD, King Nissanka Malla of Polonnaruwa banned all hunting, shooting and fishing

*Dawn on the Colombo–Kandy road (**above**). In one hour, the traffic jams will begin. The Kalawewa (**right**), King Dhatusena's pride and the chief achievement of his eighteen-year rule. He was walled up in the embankment by his son Kassapa, the builder of Sigiriya.*

within a radius of twenty-four miles from the capital. Today, Ceylon's wildlife sanctuaries cover some 6,000-odd square kilometres and vary from the Yala Strict Natural Reserve, where humans (other than accredited scientists with Conservation Department permits) are forbidden, to Uda Walawe, where a good many people actually live. The jungle, of course, is not confined to the sanctuaries, nor are its inhabitants. Often a slash-and-burn farmer will wake up in the middle of the night to the sound of elephants rampaging through the forest clearing he tends. This may end up being harder on the elephant than on the farmer, as reprisals for such rampages are one of the chief causes of the unfortunate animals' continuing persecution.

The word *sinha*, which is Sinhalese for lion, makes so many appearances in this book that the reader might be forgiven for imagining Sri Lanka to be infested with the beasts. Palaentologists have discovered fossil remains of lions, along with those of rhinoceri and hippopotami, on the island, but nowadays the only lions about the place are the Sinhalese themselves, who claim to be descended from a lion; an Indian one at that. There is no doubt that the real king of Sri Lanka's beasts is the elephant.

Alexander the Great's pilot, Onesicritos, described the Sri Lankan elephants in the 4th century BC, and the great Roman geographer Pliny quotes him as saying that they "were bigger, more fierce and furious for war service than those of India." In Pliny's time, and for many centuries thereafter, ivory represented one of Sri Lanka's major exports. Even the animals themselves were often shipped abroad, to serve with the armies of foreign potentates.

Once, elephants moved with equal freedom through the forests of the Wet Zone and the Dry Zone plains. Their liberty ended with the arrival of the White Hunter. In 1837, it is reported, a party of four Europeans killed 106 elephants in three days. A certain Major Rogers is supposed to have "bagged" more than 1,300. Rogers, a teaplanter in Badulla, could easily have grown rich on the proceeds of his slaughter, but appears to have chosen not to: his house was said to be "filled with ivory, for among the hosts of the slain were sixty tusked elephants." It seems he preferred to retain these grisly trophies rather than sell them and make a fortune. In spite of Major Rogers and his kind, elephants continue to survive in large numbers. However, men now compete with them for living-space in some parts of the Dry Zone, and their continued welfare hangs in the balance.

The Asian elephant, *Elephas maximus*, stands over three metres tall when it is fully grown and weighs between 4 and 5 tonnes. Wild ones need to be approached with caution, although usually an elephant will not charge unless it feels threatened. Exceptions are elephants in *must*, a condition that afflicts adult bulls once a year, making them savage and unpredictable even to their mahouts.

Must aside, elephants are easily domesticated, turning into docile, intelligent workers. Sri Lankans use elephants as all-purpose lifters and movers. Their capture, care and training is an old and dignified art, still valued and practised in the country; the court of Anuradhapura had a "master of elephants" as long ago as the first century BC. The ancient Sinhalese used elephants to help build the great tanks and, in addition, often employed them as tanks of the other variety in the frequent wars of the era. The decisive part played by Kandulu, King Dutugemunu's war-elephant, in one of Sri Lankan history's most crucial battles, is mentioned in a previous chapter.

In contemporary life, elephants cannot help but add spectacle to public ceremonies, in particular the Kandy Perahera, the annual exposition of the Tooth Relic of the Buddha. Every day while the festival is in full swing, a procession of the gigantic beasts, gorgeously and meticulously dressed and decorated, winds its way through the streets of the hill capital, with the most dignified old tusker of all bearing the treasured relic-casket on his back.

We went looking for wild elephants in the Bundala Sanctuary which lies on the southeast coast, near the town of Tissamaharama. We found something very different, however. The country around the Sanctuary is part of one of the island's two arid zones, areas that receive even less rainfall than the rest of the Dry Zone. It is not one of the country's more popular sanctuaries since there are no proper residential facilities, and visitors must fend very much for themselves. The lonely terrain is scratchy scrub jungle, dune and salt marsh.

After a whole day spent searching for elephants, we made our way back to camp, along the shore of a brackish lagoon. It was overcast, with a light haze through which the sun was setting in tones of rose and pearly grey, with an effect rather like that of a Chinese brush-painting. There were no shadows. Far away on the lake, a pink smudge appeared and as we drew closer, resolved itself into a flock of flamingos.

Almost before we could properly make them out, we heard them: the clamour of a gigantic family argument. There must have been at least three thousand of the birds on the water and in the air above it. Every so often a portion of the flock would take off, circle and land in a flurry of pink, black and white wing-beats. Good fortune had provided a narrow spit of firm ground reaching out into the lagoon; greatly daring, we drove slowly along it and found ourselves in the midst of a tumult of flamingos.

They utterly ignored us. We must have spent twenty minutes on that tiny headland, with the big birds gliding in to land a few feet above our heads, while the sun fell below the horizon and the sky began to darken. Eventually it was we who left, to retire to our camp and try to make sense of an event that none of us felt quite certain had actually happened.

*Flaps, airbrakes and undercarriage fully extended, a stork prepares to land. "The trouble with peacocks," says a man who keeps several, "is that they look divine and sound diabolical." The raucous dawn greeting, the dramatic landing and the Yala leopardess (**following double page**) were photographed by Luxsman Nadarajah.*

As the nights lengthen in Eurasia, the birds begin to fly south. All across the vast sweep of the continent, they rise, from the steppes of Central Europe to the Siberian tundra, from Mongolia, China and even Japan, fleeing before the steadily advancing chill. Every night the Pole Star stands a little lower on the horizon behind them, and gradually the days grow warm again. Many find hospitable feeding-grounds on the way south, but there is not enough room for all, and the rest must fare on. Below them the continent narrows, and soon they are flying down the long Deccan funnel towards the small tear-shaped island that lies at its tip. Here they must stop, or perish; the next landfall south is frozen Antarctica.

Some 150 species of migrant bird visit Sri Lanka every year, seeking shelter from the bitter cold of the northern winter. They join an indigenous population of another 250 species, of which perhaps a hundred are indigenous, found nowhere else in the world. Like Prospero's Isle in *The Tempest*, the Isle of Lanka is "full of noises": it is the noise of birdsong.

Ornithologists' descriptions of field-trips in Sri Lanka usually make for very dull reading. The sheer extravagance of the spectacle before him defeats the expert's powers of description and he is usually reduced to making lists: peacock and lapwing, kingfisher and cormorant, eagle, flycatcher and fruit-dove. It is a rare bird-fancier who can keep his head at the pageant of wings in Sri Lanka.

On the island of Delft, near Jaffna, wild ponies run. In the lagoon at Batticaloa, the fish are said to sing. You can hear them for yourself, in their season. In Trincomalee harbour, great sea-snakes skim across the water like a pebble tossed by a child.

In the days of the kings of Lanka, they say, a royal banquet often comprised so many dishes that no one could possibly have tasted them all, even if he took only a spoonful from each. You ate what you could: a morsel here, a tidbit there, of whatever looked most tempting. At the end, since it was unlikely that anyone had chosen exactly as you had done, you would have eaten of a unique feast. The wilderness of Sri Lanka is like one of those royal banquets. There is too much variety to take in all at once; one must choose carefully or be prepared to spend a lifetime at table. But whatever the choice, one thing is certain; the feast is not only unique, but fit for a king.

Plates from A History of the Birds of Ceylon, published in 1880. The illustrator, J G Keulaman portrays a Red Woodpecker, the Ceylon Mountain Hawk Eagle, Layard's Woodpecker, Ceylon Crested Falcon, Southern Golden-backed Woodpecker, Ceylon Spurfowl, Brown Wood Owl and Ceylon Bay Owl and the Ceylon jungle fowl.

These minutely-detailed paintings represent a triumph of observation. The chromolithograph prints are from A Selection of Rare and Curious Fishes Found upon the East Coast of Ceylon from Drawings Made in that Island and Coloured from Life by J W Bennet and members of the Literary and Agricultural Society of Life.

NATURE

The treasures of the land

TAKE A BOWL AND FILL IT WITH THE FRUITS of Sri Lanka. You will have to find a large bowl, for there is much to accommodate: several kinds of mangos, guavas and bananas; pineapple, papaya, grapefruit, orange; passion-fruit, pears, pomegranates; *damson*, wood-apple, *jambu*, mangosteen and lichees; sour *lovi-lovi* and *ambarella*; sweet melons; durian with their anti-social fragrance; soursop, avocado and what is probably the largest edible fruit in the world, the fifty-pound *jak*. So much for the commoner varieties; now go back and find an even larger bowl to hold the rest.

Living in the midst of such abundance, it would seem that the people of Sri Lanka must labour very little, if at all, to find their living. If this were so, it would be perfectly in keeping with the myth of the island Paradise, where the fish jump out of the sea to land at the islander's feet, and the coconuts fall out of the trees and into his lap. It sounds marvellous, but whatever dazzled visitors might think, it is not like that here. Sri Lankans must work very hard indeed, for the land will not yield up its fruits without exacting a high toll of labour.

This is especially true of the Dry Zone where so little rain falls. The scrub and bush grow well enough in the arid climate, but rice is a thirsty crop. The crucial task of providing it with enough water to make it grow has always been the people of Lanka's biggest headache, and remains so today.

Rice is the country's staple. Its cultivation is at least as old as the history of the island. Perhaps it came here with Prince Vijaya; perhaps it was here before him; nobody knows for sure. What is certain is that the spectacle of young paddy gently shifting from one soft shade of green to the next, as the wind blows here and there about the fields, has been part of the landscape of Lanka for a very long time.

To irrigate those fields, the ancient kings presided over a water management system of incredible size and complexity. It covered the entire Dry Zone of the country and brought life even to the parched lands of the southeast and northwest. At the heart of the system was the artificial reservoir or "tank" (the word comes from the Portuguese *tanque*, meaning little lake). The first tanks were small and built for storage purposes only. At this stage, they were generally local constructions, built by villagers who would dam a nearby stream to provide themselves, their animals and their crops with water. Villagers had to learn to cooperate and coordinate water flow with their neighbours up- and downstream. By the time the great capital Anuradhapura was built, the problem of managing a municipal water supply became the king's. The first two Anuradhapura tanks, the Abhayavapi and Tissawewa were built by the rulers whose names they bear, in pre-Buddhist times. So began an era of tank-building which lasted until the fall of Polonnaruwa, fifteen centuries later.

More irrigation meant more rice crops and more wealth for the royalty. What started as a patchwork of local canals and reservoirs became integrated into a single purposeful network once royalty took a hand. Streams in the hills emptied into feeder tanks on the plains below; canals connected these to other tanks farther away, and these to still others: large ones to supply the cities of Anuradhapura and later, Polonnaruwa, and smaller ones to serve the farming villages.

Some of the tanks were several hundred acres in extent. The big ones are still in use today, along with the names their makers gave them. There is Minneriya, whose builder, King Mahasena, has become identified with the local deity and is worshipped at a small shrine by the lakeside; Kalawewa, built by tragic king Dhatusena, who died walled up in its embankment by his son, the god-king Kassapa; Kantalai and Padaviya; and the greatest of them all, the gigantic Parakrama Samudra, or Sea of Parakrama, which covers 25,000 hectares of land and holds some 134.4 million cubic metres of water when full.

*Pages 88-89: Fishing boats in Weligama harbour. **Previous double page**: A friendly fisherman on the East Coast, north of Trincomalee, and a* thambili *(king-coconut) seller down a Pettah by-lane. This armful of paddy (**left**) is en route to the threshing-floor. A young carter at ease, Anuradhapura (**above**).*

Exotic vegetables like the iceberg lettuce, can be found in the weekly markets upcountry. Vegetables are often more important than meat as the centrepieces in Sri Lanka's cuisine.

As impressive as the tanks themselves were the canals that connected them. In his lyrical *Jungle Tide*, John Still writes that he met a modern engineer who, tapping an ancient irrigation channel to supply some fields below it, had:

> "made a level survey..., selected three spots where he cut into the bank a king had built about four hundred years after Christ, and in two of the three pits he dug came upon the ruins of Sinhalese sluices; so they must have made their level surveys too, and plotted them to a yard of his..."

From Stills' description, the stream sounds like the Yodha Ela, the 54-mile channel King Dhatusena built to carry water from the Kalawewa to Anuradhapura. The Yodha Ela supplied 60 tanks and 100 villages on its route to the city. Throughout its course, it maintained a gradient of six inches to every mile. Yet it, like the rest of the tank and canal system, was designed by men who had no theodolites, nor any of the precision instruments of the modern surveyor; and it was built by human muscles, its stones carried and set in their places by straining human backs, with elephants to help the heavier work along. There were no cranes, no bulldozers, no backhoes; but the job was done and finished to a degree of exactness modern engineers have often wondered at.

The manpower for these enterprises was obtained through the system of *rajakariya*, a kind of corvée or taxation by labour where, in exchange for land tenure, farmers had to put in a certain amount of time on public works at the king's behest. The *rajakariya* system, or something like it, also obtained in time of war, when the "king's work" took the form of military service, and bands of men roamed the country, often destroying the very tanks and canals they had helped build in peacetime. Reconstructing the network would then become the task of the next monarch, once the kingdom was safely united under his rule.

It worked well enough until Polonnaruwa fell. After that, the Sinhalese retreated into the wetter lands of the southwest, where irrigation was not so much of a problem, and the tank system fell into disuse. Soon its only beneficiaries were the elephant and buffalo and the rest of the citizenry of the jungle, for as man abandoned these lands, the forest returned, to cover the old sluices and reservoirs, spread itself over the

*After the rice is harvested: a boy and his buffalo in the cleared field (**above left**), "chaffy grain beneath the thresher's flail" at Tissamaharama (**bottom left**), and a working lunch during rehearsals for the Kandy Perahera, which is usually held just after the rice harvest. **Following double page**: Upland rice paddies near Kandy.*

buildings that surrounded them, and pull them down stone by stone. Nowadays, walking in what looks to the untrained eye like virgin forest, one may often come upon a grassy, tree-filled depression, an inscribed stone or a few stumps of pillars, and learn from these things that men once walked, and spoke, and slept, where now only bird-calls and the trill of insects resound in the jungle afternoon.

The age of tanks has come and gone, but the endless cycle of sowing and harvest continues. The land bears two rice harvests a year, one, the *maha* crop, in August (around the time of the Kandy Perahera), and the other, the *yala*, in March. Although mechanisation is widespread, it is still quite usual to see a paddy-farmer tilling his fields with a plough drawn by yoked buffaloes, as his forefathers did; and the rituals surrounding the sowing, transplanting and weeding of the fields remain very much the same. Harvesting the grain is still done communally in many villages, and the farmer will still walk three times round the threshing floor, pausing at each point of the compass, to pay homage to the bountiful gods before setting to work on his newly-harvested grain. The straw men who stood watch in the fields while his crop ripened were not scarecrows; they were there to ward off the Evil Eye.

There is another sort of traditional agriculture that is practised in Sri Lanka, and it is as old as, if not older than, wet rice cultivation. This is the slash-and-burn method, where forest clearings are cut and planted, the ash serving as fertilizer. It is barely profitable work, for the plot has to be cleared, planted and guarded against raids by wild animals. The pulses, dry rice and other crops the farmer sows bring in very little money; as a result, the slash-and-burn cultivator is the poorest of those who work the land. After the ripe crop is harvested, he must move on to another clearing, because this method of farming so depletes the soil that it will not bear again next year. The wild scrub re-occupies the abandoned plot soon enough, but the trees the farmer has cut down are not so easily replaced. Slash-and-burn farming is now officially discouraged, but not very actively, since it is many people's only means of livelihood.

If slash-and-burn farming is unprofitable, another, much more recent, form of agriculture has proved to be its very opposite. The cultivation of tea has made fortunes, elevated generations of middle-class Britons to the rank of minor potentates and still provides the bulk of Sri Lanka's foreign earnings. It has also, for better or worse, changed the landscape of the hill country forever. Before tea, there was coffee. Kandy was taken by the British in 1815. Eight years later, the first coffee plantations were clinging to the hill-slopes around the fallen Sinhalese capital. The British had seen the potential of those hillsides and, with empire-building energy, set out quickly to exploit it.

They were proved right in their expectations. The coffee-shrubs thrived, and soon a rush was on for the precious land. Acre upon acre of priceless first-growth forest rang with what one observer described as the "merry chime" of axes. Ships left Colombo heavily laden with countless tons of coffee, to meet the growing demands of a Europe now hooked on coffee. And then, in 1869, the Great Blight began.

D M Forrest, in his authoritative *A Hundred Years of Ceylon Tea*, calls *Hemileia vastatrix*, the coffee-rust fungus, the "patron saint of the tea industry". In 1870, a year after it appeared, sales of coffee reached their peak. After that, the fungus settled in, and the end of King Coffee was in sight.

Luckily, another crop was ready to replace it. There is some dispute over who exactly introduced *Camellia sinensis* to Ceylon. But there are no arguments over who was first to plant it commercially. At Mahaiyawa Cemetery in Kandy, there is a gravestone erected:

"*In pious memory of James Taylor, Loolecon-dera Estate, Ceylon, the pioneer of the tea... enterprise, who died May 2, 1892, aged 57 years.*"

It is said that James Taylor weighed two hundred and forty-six pounds and could knock a man over with one finger. However, a photograph of him dated 1864 shows someone far less heroically proportioned. Perhaps he grew heavy in later life, during the long, reclusive years he spent at Loolecondera. Still, so great a bulk becomes his memory well; to the planters of Ceylon, Taylor is a giant.

The son of a Scotch wheelwright, he came to Ceylon in 1841, to work for a Mr George Pride of Kandy. Loolecondera was his second coffee plantation, high on an inhospitable mountain ridge where the wind blew "a perfect hurricane" and the temporary bunga-low he occupied was overrun with rats. However,

Taylor was happy enough; he meant to "make a go of it", and besides, there were compensations. In a letter home to Laurencekirk, he wrote: "You will think I write a lot about the scenery, but if you saw it you would not think I said too much."

In 1867, Taylor planted No.7 field at Loolecondera with tea seeds he obtained from the Royal Botanic Gardens in Peradeniya. The experiment was authorised and paid for by his employers, but it was he who had to make the new plant grow. It meant learning how to do what had never been done before on the island. The methodical Scot set to work with the same dedication he brought to everything else he did, and the experiment was a success. The seeds grew into bushes that produced fine tea.

For Taylor and for Ceylon, it was just the beginning. The superintendent of Loolecondera became an authority on tea by the far from simple process of doing it all first, and doing it right: cultivation, processing and all the rest; inventing methods and procedures as he went along. And where he led, a host of others followed, to reap the green gold of the mountains.

The hill country of Sri Lanka is dotted with signboards that must have given some comfort to homesick British planters. Scotland is strongly represented: there are Glasgow and Gleneagles, St. Andrews and a score of other Scottish names. There is an Eton in the hills, and a Harrow too. There are Mayfair and Belgravia, Sherwood and Avon. The names of the tea plantations, or estates, tell us something about the men who planted them and laboured to make them grow.

They were a rough enough crew at first, hardy pioneers whose lives were constant hardship; but soon conditions changed. Taylor's successors were kings in their own domain, and they began to behave accordingly. In the early days, the planter often occupied "a miserable little cabin... not more than twelve feet long by about six feet wide". Less than two decades after Taylor's experiment, however, a visitor to "a very remote plantation" was "given very clearly to understand that my host expected to see me at dinner in a black tail coat and white tie."

Contemporary planters live somewhat differently. During the socialist government of Mrs Sirima Bandaranaike in 1972, the estates, still largely British-owned, were nationalised. Two government bodies were created to manage them, and the superintendents became employees of the state.

By then, the era of tie-and-tails to dinner had long since passed, anyhow, and life in the plantation bungalows had become much like middle-class living anywhere else in the country. As for the estate workers, the impoverished Tamils whose grandparents had been lured over from India by promises of gold to live and work in utmost squalor, their lives have improved a little, though in this area there remains much to be done. The 'coolie lines', cramped dormitories where the labourers live, are still with us; it will be

To feed this limekiln and hundreds of others, large areas of the West Coast coral reef have been destroyed; now, in a tragic display of poetic justice, sea erosion is washing away the coralminers' homes.

a happy day for the country when the last one is torn down, and its occupants better housed.

The story of tea, in a slightly less dramatic fashion, repeats itself in the tale of the country's second commercial crop, rubber. Rubber and coconut are the other two legs of Sri Lanka's export economy, which is still as strongly based on agriculture as it was in colonial times. It is not the soundest basis for a national economy, and countless attempts have been made to augment the Big Three with other, more value-added exports. These have met with varying degrees of success and continue to hold promise, but commercial agriculture still dominates the economy, and tea still reigns supreme, from the mountain fastness where, a hundred and twenty years ago, it succeeded coffee as King of crops.

A European company director, head of the Sri Lankan branch of a large multinational firm, is puzzled. He cannot understand why, despite the best efforts of his sales force and his advertising agency, the product his company markets will sell no more than a token few hundred cases a year. A lot of money has been spent trying to "educate the consumer" to buy his product. Why won't it sell?

Part of the reason, of course, is that Sri Lanka is still a very poor country, and the expatriate's product is, to most of her people, a luxury they can make do without. But there is another reason, one which he cannot quite bring himself to accept, and can scarcely

understand. It is this: for two-thousand-odd years, the people of Lanka have lived in an intimate relationship with the land. It provided them with all they needed, and their whole social organisation was based upon it. Ninety-five out of a hundred Sinhalese were farmers. Hereditary craftsmen, soldiers, even courtiers, all tilled their own lands; the very sons of dukes themselves descended into the fields.

Each village was self-sufficient, except for salt and a tiny handful of luxuries. There was no commerce in the modern sense. Money itself was largely unknown.

And, to the surprise of the expatriate, it is much the same today. They may not last any longer, for the marketing wizard and his colleagues are doing their best to eradicate them; but the old links with the land, the ties that the Industrial Revolution severed in the West (and the media revolution is now destroying in the lands of the Far East) are still very strong in Sri Lanka. As long as these links remain, the only market for the expatriates' products, apart from a few demonstrably useful things, like soap, will be among the confused folk of the big city.

Sri Lanka is, yet, unspoilt. The word evokes visions of childlike natives ripe for exploitation, beaming happily up at the Great Despoiler; but that, like so many facets of the Paradise myth, does not fit Sri Lanka. This is an old country, long civilised, often invaded, and her people remember. Turning them into mere consumers will not be an easy task.

*Relief for a thousand heavy-headed Colombo commuters comes with a draught of sweet king-coconut water (**above**). This porter (**right**) at Pettah market, Colombo, won't suffer from that particular problem. **Following double page**: contour-planted tea blankets the hill country. The crop provides the bulk of Sri Lanka's export earnings.*

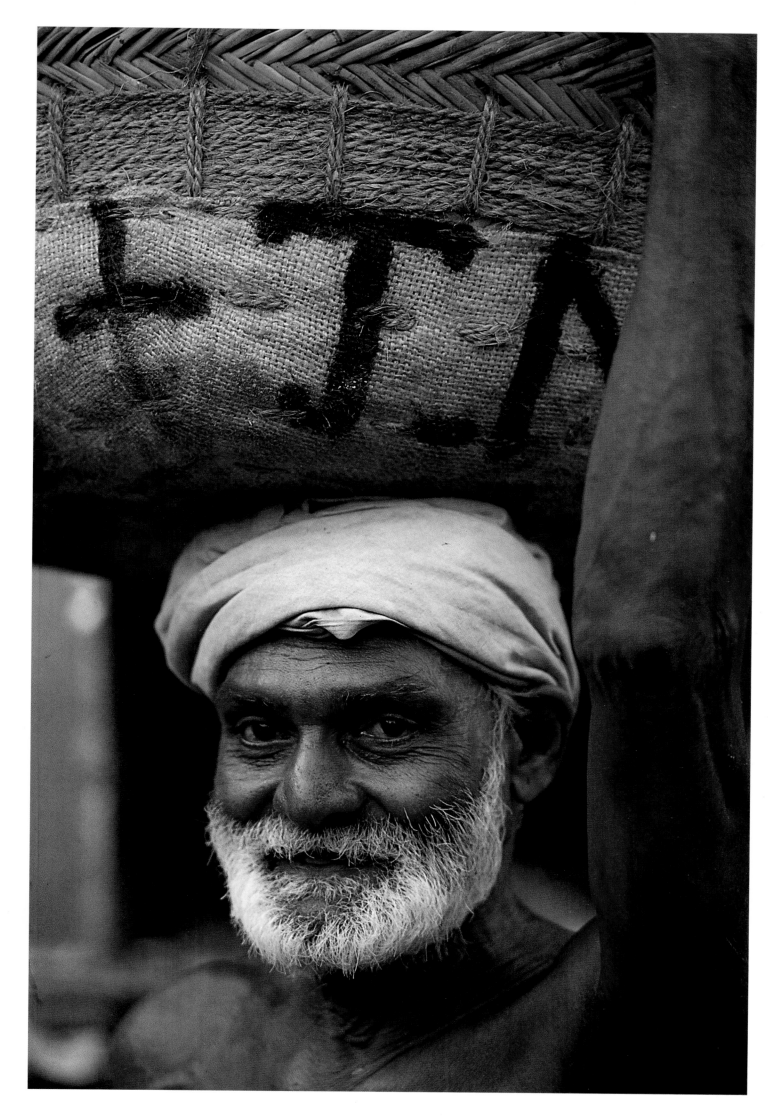

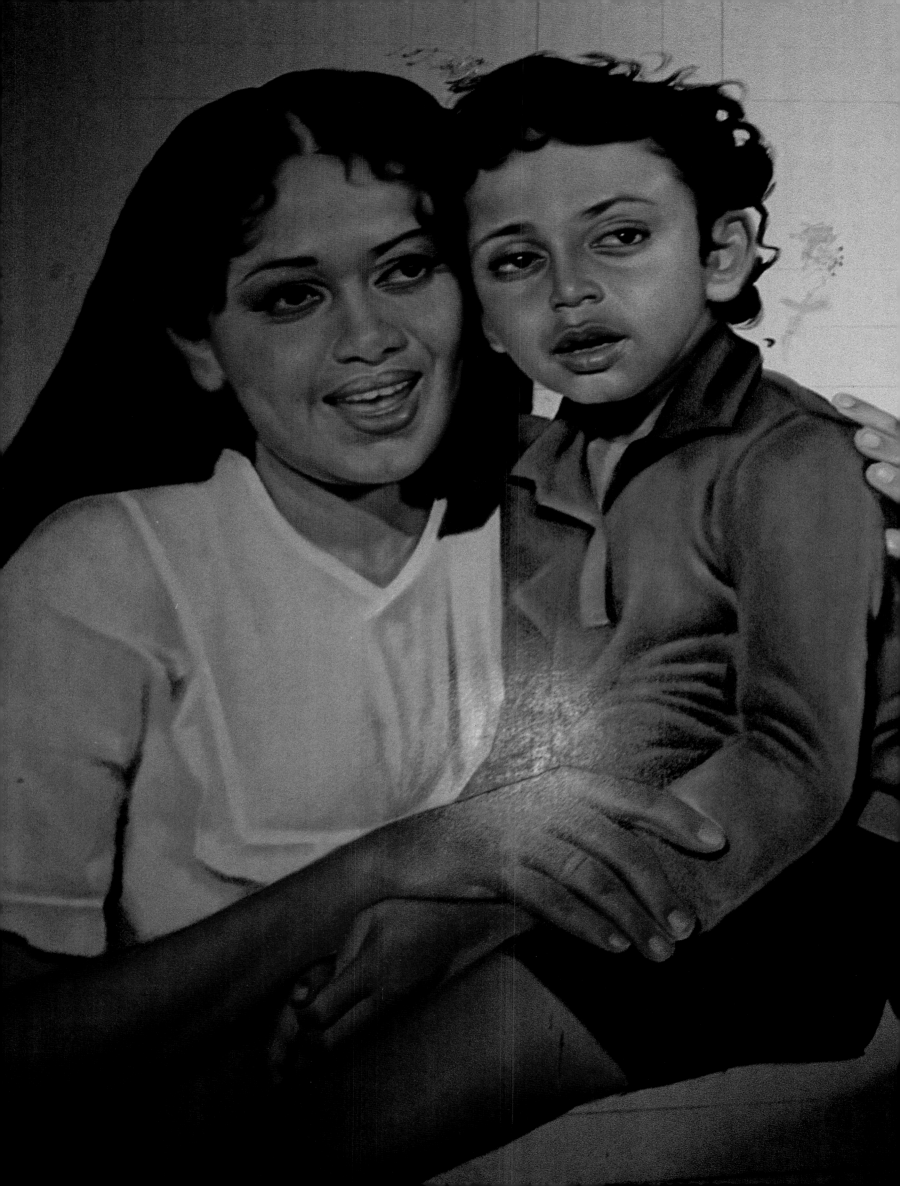

STYLES
The textures of daily life

IT GROWS ALMOST TEDIOUS, THIS INSISTENCE on variety. Yet there is no escaping it, for whichever aspect of Sri Lanka you examine — fauna or flora, food or folklore — the story is always the same: incredible complexity and profusion. Nothing is ever simple or uniform here, and surprises lie in wait round every corner. Sri Lanka is a wonderful country to experience, but a terribly difficult one to try to describe. Anthropologists in particular have a hard time of it. Nominally speaking, the island's 15 million inhabitants are divided into four ethnic groups and a tiny fifth category labelled 'others'. However this is really just a sketchy outline, for intermarriage (and cohabitation) have long since blurred many of the distinctions between the groups; and to complicate things even more, each encompasses a host of different cultural and ethnic strains. 2,500 years at the crossroads of trade have left an ineradicable mark.

Three languages are spoken. Sinhala, the language of the majority, is the first of these. Tamil is the second language of the country, spoken by sizeable minorities (Ceylon Tamils, Indian Tamils and Ceylon Muslims). The third, the language of commerce and of the westernised, urban middle class, is English. Although the latter is 'mother tongue' only to the dwindling Burgher minority, the British influence lingers still, and even in rural districts it is usually possible to find someone who understands the language and perhaps speaks in a close approximation of the British Queen's cadence. For the visitor, it is often the only constant factor in the kaleidoscope that whirls around him.

There has always been some debate about who actually settled the island first; the Sinhalese dominate the historical record. The controversy arouses unseemly passions, so we will not involve ourselves with it; at all events, if anyone has a prior claim on the Isle of Lanka, it is the fast-disappearing remnant of the island's indigenous inhabitants, the Veddas.

Like most ancient things in Sri Lanka, the origin of the Veddas is attached to a legend. The story goes that when Prince Vijaya, the mythical ancestor of the Sinhalese, took an Indian wife, he rejected the *yakkhini* Kuveni, the native woman (or demoness, or dryad) whom he had lived with before. Kuveni returned to Lankapura, the home of her race, but was killed by her own people. Her children, brother and sister, fled to safety and later founded the race of tribal peoples referred to in the *Mahavamsa* as the Pulindas. The Veddas are said to be their present-day descendants.

In fact, the Veddas probably antedate Vijaya and Kuveni. No one knows where they came from; sources such as Australasia, Africa and the Mediterranean have been mentioned. They do not seem to be from the same racial or genetic stock as the Sinhalese and Tamils. But there have been men on this island practically forever, and origins are not easy to trace.

Robert Knox, an English prisoner of the King of Kandy who lived among the Sinhalese for nineteen years during the late 19th century, described the Veddas of his time as follows:

"The land of Bintenne is covered with mighty woods, filled with an abundance of deer. Here are found the wild men called Veddahs, who live apart from the other inhabitants, but speak the Chingulay's (Sinhalese) language. They kill deer and dry the flesh over the fire... They do not till any ground for corn, their food being confined to flesh and fish when they can catch it. They are therefore, very expert with their bows; they use a little axe fastened to their sides, to cut honey out of hollow trees... generally speaking, they have neither towns nor houses, but live by the rivers under trees..."

Knox was describing the true 'wild' Veddas, classic hunter-gatherers of a sort found the world over. Perhaps in his time the *gam* Veddas, who practise a

*Preceding pages: This Colombo sign-painter is at work on a large cinema hoarding panel showing Malani Fonseka, by far the most popular Sinhalese film actress. As beautiful, if less glamorous, are these young Sinhalese girls (**left** and **above**).*

primitive form of forest-clearing agriculture, did not exist. By the time the Veddas were subjected to the attentions of modern anthropologists, however, primitive agriculturists were definitely in the majority. They now dwelt in stick-and-bark huts next to their *chena* clearings and wore loincloths rather than girdles of leaf and bark. But they still maintained clan laws rigidly and still worshipped their ancestral spirits.

Primitive cultures rarely survive the impact of collision with more powerful ones and even in Knox's day the Veddas were beginning to feel the benefits and burdens of civilisation. Even as the present volume is written, the last of them are being assimilated into the "civilised" population, as their tribal lands feel the thrust of development.

Practically speaking, this is for the best, for the old tribal life was hard and dangerous and its survival into the present day an anachronism; but the Veddas are not unconscious of their ancient and dignified heritage, and the process of detribalisation sometimes sits hard with them. There is a lot to be said for the freedom of the forest and the taste of venison cured in honey.

Three-quarters of the population of Sri Lanka is Sinhalese, and nearly all of them are Buddhists. The history of Sri Lanka and the history of the Sinhalese people are often taken as one and the same thing. This is because the great Sinhalese chronicles, the *Mahavamsa* and *Culavamsa*, are so complete and, in matters of chronology and detail, so accurate, that it is easy to forget they only tell one part of the story. However, their accuracy makes them excellent guide-posts to most of the major events in the country's early history. They also highlight the intimate relationship between the Sinhalese and Buddhism that has endured since the 3rd century BC.

One could say that Buddhism literally took root here. Siddharta Gautama received the enlightenment that transformed him into the Buddha under a *peepul* or bo-tree. Shortly after Buddhism arrived in Sri Lanka, so did a cutting of the sacred tree, borne here by Sangamitta, daughter of the Indian emperor Asoka. The bo-tree still survives in Anuradhapura. It is the oldest documented living thing in the world; its Indian ancestor, sadly, perished long ago.

Buddhism is not really a religion. It contains no accounts of creation, no gods to worship and no commandments to keep or break. You could call it

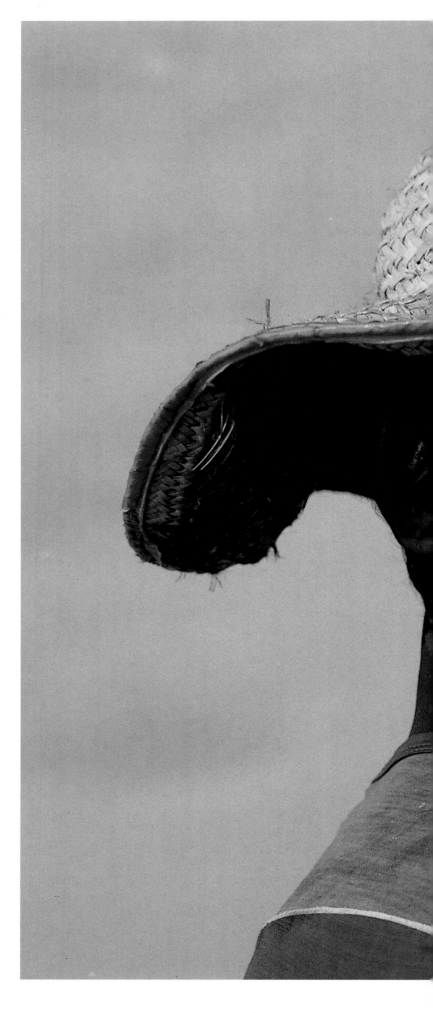

*Cocky and cool in the tropical heat, a Negombo fisherman takes his
beedi break. Beedis are small cigarettes wrapped in tobacco leaf,
popular throughout the Subcontinent.*

humanism raised to the highest power, except that it even denies the existence of the individual self.

Instead, Sakyamuni, the Buddha, taught the Four Noble Truths: that the world is full of suffering, that this suffering is caused by desire or attachement to the things of the world, that suffering would cease when attachment did and that this result could be achieved by following eight simple but demanding rules: the so-called Middle Way. The relationship between attachment and suffering, he explained as being part of the law of action and reaction, or karma. It is all very logical and unmysterious; it is also terribly uncompromising. There are no shortcuts to liberation, which can only be won through one's own efforts. It is not a religion for the weak-minded.

This is the philosophy that has moulded Sinhalese culture since ancient times. It explains the simplicity and austerity that run through every facet of that culture. It repeats itself in everything from the design of giant stupas to the architecture of a farmer's house, from the ceremonies of Poson and Vesak to the everyday rituals of hearth and home.

According to the Buddha, striving is the result of desire and is therefore futile. Robert Knox noted, of his Sinhalese captors, that "riches are not here valued, nor make any the more honourable." The novelist Martin Wickramasinghe, in *Aspects of Sinhalese Culture*, points out that many folk rhymes also reflect the Buddhist attitude, which sees loss and gain as inevitable and equally meaningless:

"Tired, I came to the travellers' rest
Lugging my pans and pots,
And all I could do was laugh and laugh
When a bullock smashed the lot."

On the other hand, while striving for personal gain was considered futile, efforts devoted to the service of others would, through the action of karma, help one along the path to liberation. Charity, or *dana*, is the foremost of the Buddhist virtues. Its most endearing expression in Sri Lanka is the *pinthaliya*, a water-pot and dipper placed by the roadside for thirsty travellers. The *pinthali* are acts of personal charity; the *ambalama*, the "travellers' rest" mentioned in the rhyme, was usually built at the king's behest.

Of all forms of charity, the highest is *sanghadana*, charity offered to the Buddhist clergy, for the monks depend strictly upon it for food, clothing, medicine and shelter, and are expected to require nothing more (this, at any rate, is the principle). *Dana* is given only by invitation. With the sacred relic of their temple borne high before them on the head of one of their hosts, the monks are conducted in procession to the place where they will be fed and entertained. They walk under a cloth canopy, accompanied by drummers who go before them to act as heralds.

A sheet of white cloth covers the approach to their host's house. He will greet them at the door with both hands clasped in front of his face and conduct them to the special seats prepared for them. The rest of the company will usually sit on the floor, for to the Sinhalese, a high seat is a mark of honour.

After they are seated, the monks extend their begging-bowls into which the food is served. After eating, they are offered betel leaves for chewing, and conducted back to the temple. The ceremonies are essentially over before noon, for all solid food is prohibited to the monks after that time.

A word or two needs to be said about caste. In modern Sri Lanka, the Sinhalese caste system retains its grip in only two areas: marriage and politics. In the latter, low caste can be a serious handicap to an electoral candidacy. In the former, it is one of many factors involved in the selection of partners.

Basically, caste is the division of society into classes according to occupation and sometimes religious status. To be effective, it presupposes the handing down of craft skills and traditions from father to son, or at least between successive generations of an extended family. As soon as that mechanism falters, religious rationales lose their power, and the caste system becomes obsolete.

It has been said that the Sri Lankan caste system, unlike its Indian counterpart, did not exalt one caste over another. This may have been true of antiquity, but by the end of the Kandyan period, a definite stratification had taken place. The *Janavamsa*, a 15th-century Sinhalese poem, lists no less than 26 castes in order of precedence, from farmers to scavengers. At least ten of these were active components of eighteenth-century Kandyan society.

Oddly enough, the highest of all Sinhalese castes is the *govi*, or farmer, caste. There could be no hereditary priesthood in a Buddhist country, and warriors did not constitute a sizeable caste, so except

for the royal family, the *goviya* was pre-eminent. Nor was this simply a matter of form; the cultivators took their precedence very seriously. An old Sinhalese proverb has it that any ploughman, washed clean of the mud from his paddy-field, is fit to rule the kingdom, and Robert Knox observed that there was "no difference between the ability and speech of a country-man and a courtier." To make the situation even more paradoxical, more than nine out of ten Kandyans belonged to the farmers' caste!

Arguments and even representations to the courts on matters of caste precedence were common occurrences some years ago, but the issue seems to be dead now. However, its survival over the centuries, in the face of Buddhism (which does not recognise castes) is proof of its tenacity, and it may yet be too early to write its overdue epitaph.

Though caste plays a role in the selection of marital partners, the wedding ceremony itself is essentially the same for all Sinhalese. Even today, the great majority of Sinhalese marriages are arranged. Parents with marriageable sons and daughters become part of a proposal network that includes relatives, friends and often a professional match-maker, the *magul kapuwa*. Many families find the services of a professional useful, for there is much to be discussed and settled: horoscopes to compare, the dowry to be agreed upon and so on. Once all the preliminaries are over, the betrothal can take place.

The core of this ceremony is the reading of a document, by the bridegroom-to-be, which lists the auspicious times for the conduct of all activities pertaining to the wedding, from baking the sweet-meats to the actual *poruwa* ceremony itself. The reading takes place at the bride's house and is attended by relatives of both parties. The formalities end with an exchange of rings.

The focal point of the actual wedding ceremony is the *poruwa*. This is a raised dais, decorated with flowers and flanked by *gokkola* (young coconut palm) decorations. The floor is draped with white cloth and strewn with rice. There are also items of food on the *poruwa*, which is covered with a white canopy.

The wedding itself is hosted by the bride's family, usually at home (though hotel ballrooms are in vogue amongst those who can afford them). The groom arrives, dressed in white and accompanied by a procession of relatives. His feet are washed (usually a ceremonial sprinkling) by the bride's brother or a stand-in. The groom then awaits the auspicious moment at which his bride appears, and they step on to the *poruwa* together. They then exchange gifts, traditionally clothing, and the groom places an elaborate necklace of worked gold about the girl's neck. Various minor ceremonies follow while the assembled company waits impatiently for the climax.

This occurs when the bride's uncle ties the couple's right thumbs together with a piece of gold

A banana leaf makes poor shelter from the heavy rains of the Southwest monsoon.

thread. Water is then poured over the knot. This is the nuptial moment. The custom is the same in Hindu marriages; the pouring of water signifies transfer of property. The reader can decide exactly what is being transferred, and to whom.

A coconut is split open upon the *poruwa* for luck, and then it is all over, bar the shouting — which takes the form of *Jayamangala Gatha*, a traditional benediction, and a final flourish of drums. The actual wedding concluded, everybody sits down to a sumptuous meal, after which the couple take their leave; for the bridegroom's home or, in the case of more contemporary-minded newlyweds, off on honeymoon.

In present-day Sri Lanka, the Tamils form the largest of the minorities. They fall into two groups: the Sri Lanka or Jaffna Tamils and the so-called 'Indian' Tamils. The latter are a more recent addition to the nation's ethnic mix: they are the descendants of the South Indian labourers brought to Sri Lanka by the British to work the tea plantations, and most of them are still employed thus. Their present standing in Sri Lanka is uncertain. Many of them are technically stateless and so, do not have a vote or any of the official rights of a Sri Lankan citizen. They constitute approximately eight percent of the country's population and are concentrated mostly in the central hills, the tea country.

The more settled Tamils are a much larger minority: about 13 percent. For the most part, they live in the North and East of the island, although the Puttalam area in the north-west and of course the capital Colombo, also have sizeable Tamil communities. The centre of Sri Lankan Tamil culture is the peninsula of Jaffna, at the northern end of the island. Jaffna's proximity to India (the distance is only 48 kilometres) has meant close ties between the two since antiquity, and the people of Jaffna share many ways with their Indian cousins. However, Jaffna is not Tamilnadu or Kerala writ small; the peninsula has its own unique and distinct culture.

Although we know that the original Jaffna Tamils came from South India, the date of the first migrations is uncertain. Legend has it that one of them, a wandering minstrel of the Panan clan, landed in Lanka and went to sing at the royal court, accompanying himself on the *yal*, a stringed instrument somewhere between a lute and a harp. His performance pleased and intrigued the king, who questioned the minstrel closely and tested the extrasensory powers he claimed to possess. The minstrel, whose name by one account was Vira Raghavan, passed the examination and was awarded a parcel of land on which to settle.

One version of the legend has it that the king who made the award was the Tamil ruler of Jaffna, and the land a dry, sandy portion of that kingdom; another claims that the king was the ruler of all Lanka, and the award was the Jaffna peninsula itself. To this day, the Tamil name for the peninsula is Yalpanam or Yalpanapattinam, and the Bishop of Jaffna carries a harp on his coat-of-arms.

Like the story of Vijaya, the legend of the Panan minstrel symbolises a wave of migrations to Lanka. The port of Mantota flourished in ancient times, and despite upheavals over the centuries, the Jaffna traders managed to maintain their lucrative trade and sustain a stable and lasting way of life.

In the ninth century, a Kalingan prince (or a crook claiming to be one) rose to power in Jaffna. His name was Uggirasingham. The Kalingan line of succession he founded evolved over time into the Arya Chakravarti dynasty. Although the early history of the line is obscure, the Chakravarties eventually established themselves as the greatest of Jaffna's ruling houses, and after the early 13th century, the Chakravarti succession was interrupted only once before its final overthrow by the Portuguese in 1620. The interruption was caused by an attack on Jaffna in 1450 by King Parakramabahu VI of Kotte. Jaffna fell and was occupied by the Sinhalese for 17 years. But on the whole, such wars between Sinhalese monarchs and the Tamil kings of Jaffna seem to have been rare; the violence came from conflicts with the periodic expansionism of the Tamil kingdoms of South India.

The Arya Chakravarti succession continued for a while under the Portuguese hegemony. But the puppets insisted on pulling their own strings. After 70 years of power struggles and civil unrest, the pretence of independence was dropped once and for all. The last of the kings of Jaffna was deposed, and the kingdom annexed to Portugal.

Thus ended the independent kingdom of Jaffna. The peninsula remained in Portuguese hands until 1658. Towards the middle of the 18th century, the Dutch steadily began eroding the territory controlled

by the Portuguese, and Sri Lanka eventually passed into their hands. The Dutch held the country for little more than a century, but in those years they developed Jaffna as their main port. In 1796, the Dutch surrendered Jaffna without a fight to an over-whelmingly strong British force. With the fall of the last independent kingdom of Kandy in the south in 1815, Jaffna came under the general British administration, the first time the peninsula was governed as a integral part of the rest of the island.

A famous writer once called the Coromandel peoples 'leaping Tamils'. The inelegant phrase was intended as a compliment, a tribute to their energy and industry. The Tamils of Sri Lanka certainly display both qualities in abundance. It has been said that the land shapes their character, for Jaffna is dry and not naturally fertile. It is hard to make anything grow there, but the Jaffna farmer prospers by ingenuity and effort, pumping water from deep wells to quench the thirsty red soil. Jaffna is Sri Lanka's vegetable-garden. The peninsula even boasts vineyards, tended by Rosarian monks at Tholagatty.

All Tamils do not live in Jaffna, nor are all Jaffna's Tamils farmers; perhaps Tamil industry is not so glibly explained. Whatever its cause, that industry, together with thrift and a passion for learning, have given Tamils a strong presence in business, civil administration and the professions. The community also has a long and highly distinguished academic tradition.

Hinduism shapes Tamil culture just as Buddhism does Sinhalese. The *kovil* is a pivotal presence in every Tamil community. The faith enshrined there is not an easy one to describe. Hinduism postulates a single creative essence, known as Brahma. The 'Original Divinity' has three aspects: Brahma, the Creator, Visnu, the Preserver, and Siva, the Destroyer. From this great trinity a huge and complex pantheon arises, gods and goddesses whose aspects and manifestations blend into one another to form an endless tapestry of divinities. All of reality, both inner and outer, is pictured in it.

As a result, there are almost as many forms of Hinduism as there are Hindus. There is the high philosophy of the Veddas, there is the simple folk religion of the tea plantation workers, and there are innumerable levels of complexity in between. Sects that emphasise peace and transcendence coexist with cults that demand self-flagellation or blood sacrifice.

Sri Lankan Hinduism is of the Saiva Siddhanta or Saivite school, dedicated to the worship of Siva and the complex of divinities emanating from him. Saivaism is one of the two main streams of modern Hindu worship (the other, Vaisnava, dedicated to Visnu, is more popular in North India than in the South). Siva is the Destroyer, but his cult is not a negative one; destruction, after all, is only the prelude to a new creation and thus, a necessary component of the unending cosmic cycle; so Siva is Nataraja, Lord of The

A guarded smile from a Sinhalese girl at Kataragama.

Amid all the political turmoil that surrounds them, Sri Lankans must be among the world's friendliest peoples.

*These young fortune-tellers (**above**) represent yet another side of Sri Lanka's varied population. Pale hair swirls around the ash-streaked forehead of an old Hindu devotee (**right**).*

Dance, whose dancing continually makes and unmakes the world. The four-armed Nataraja, dancing in a circle of flame, is one of the most compelling images of divinity ever wrought by man.

All great religions must justify God's ways to man; in other words, explain the scheme of things to the believer. Most achieve this by means of a set of broad principles, flexible enough to accommodate the world (or most of it). Hinduism goes into detail, laying emphasis on the *act* of worhip. As a result, Tamil life is set about by elaborate customs and observances. Every one of them has a symbolic meaning, but this is not always readily understood.

In societies where marriage by arrangement is the custom, coming-of-age rites signify a young woman's eligibility to wed. They are usually significant family events. When a Tamil girl of the *vellala* caste attains puberty, she goes into seclusion for up to a month, attended by a woman of a lower caste. The day, month and time of the event are noted, and astrology texts consulted to determine their significance. Changing of clothes becomes a solemn daily ceremony. She is fitted with silver toe-rings. Her protectress, the *koviyar* woman, carries a handful of *margosa* and palmyrah leaves and a small *satthakam*, or dagger.

Taking a bath becomes a major operation, in which she is assisted by her protectress and any number of girl-cousins. Clothes and all jewellery are removed, and the girl is seated on a mat of *cadjan* thatch. She holds three betel-leaves, three areca nuts and a coin. A tray bearing a tuft of grass, a pot of milk and another of water are near at hand. Camphor is lit, and the bath can take place.

Throughout her seclusion, the girl cannot so much as glimpse a man, not even a father or brother. At the end of the month, the girl takes her place in adult society. Robed in silk, bejewelled, she is conducted in procession to the room where the ceremony is to be held. She walks on a white cloth; attendants hold a canopy over her head. She takes her seat, facing a pot of water. Eleven times, objects are waved before her: cooked food, fruit and flowers, curds, a coin. This is to counteract malefic forces to which young women are thought to be susceptible. There is also a practical side to the proceedings, for the *arathi* is performed by aunts who might have an eligible son or two on hand.

Caste assumes a comparatively large role in Tamil life, though here too, much has changed lately. For the record, Tamils do have a priestly, or Brahmin, caste, but in Sri Lanka only the *kovil* priests belong to this caste, and precedence over the farmer caste is usually waived. The *vellala*, or farmers, are the equivalent of the Sinhalese *govi* caste and like them, form a majority. Several other castes come after the *vellala* in precedence. According to tradition, the lowest of these may not eat at the same table as their superiors, nor worship the high gods in the temple.

Progressive Tamils are at the forefront of the movement to abolish what remains of these ancient inequities. They face the obstacle of conservatism, but the old barriers are crumbling and will soon be gone. In the end, there will be few to mourn them.

On the fourteenth day of the month of Muharram, in the year 682 of the Islamic calendar, an outlandish embassy arrived in the splendid city of Bhagdad. The ambassadors presented the Caliph with a golden casket. Inside it was a sheaf of palm-leaves, inscribed with writing that no one at court could read. The ambassadors obligingly translated. The document turned out to be a formal salutation from the King of Lanka to the Caliph, proposing the exchange of embassies and a trade agreement. Among the articles offered for sale were pearls, precious stones, fine woods, cinnamon and elephants.

The year was 1283 AD by Western reckoning, and Sri Lanka was already an established port of call for

Arab traders. As the power of the Malabar states waned, Muslim seafarers began to dominate the region's trade. Some of these were themselves Malabar Indians, converts to Islam whose language and culture were still predominantly Tamil; others came from the faraway lands of the Middle East. Even in the 13th century, the latter were by no means newcomers. According to the historian H.W. Codrington, the first Sri Lankan Muslims were "descendants of that portion of the Arabs of the House of Hashim who were driven out of Arabia in the 8th century by the tyranny of Caliph Abdul Malik ben Merwan." The exiles settled at several points along the island's coast; it was probably they who founded the city of Kolontota, which the Portuguese were later to name Colombo.

Sri Lanka has a special place in Arab (and Muslim) tradition. It is said to have been the home of Adam, who did penance here for a thousand years following his banishment from Paradise. There is a tradition that he is buried, along with Eve, at Talaimannar. Cain's and Abel's tombs, incidentally, are said to be at nearby Rameswaram. Of course, there is no shortage of locations claiming to be the last resting-place of the ancestral couple (the most famous of Eve's tombs is probably the one outside old Jiddah). All the same, the story illustrates just how large the isle of Serendib bulked in the imaginations of those early adventurers, who had exchanged a desert of sand for the even wider wastes of ocean.

The prototype of all those adventurous explorers was, of course, Sindbad the Sailor. The endlessly daring merchant never identified the countries he visited, but enchanted readers of the *Thousand And One Nights* have tried to do so ever since, poring over the text in search of clues. Sindbad's catalogue of wonders yields very little in the way of hard fact, but some scholars claim to see, in the vale of Ratnapura (Sinhalese for 'City of Gems'), Sindbad's Valley of Diamonds. Ratnapura today is a prosperous gemmining town, with a large Muslim business community. Its location at the southwestern approach to the hill country fits the Arabian Nights description, but the deadly snakes and giant rocs are, fortunately, nowhere in evidence. The analogy ends here.

There is an abundance of legend and story about the Muslims of Sri Lanka, but when it comes to history, the harvest is not nearly so rich. We do not know very much about the communities that grew and developed in Lanka as the centuries passed. Only tantalising fragments remain: Ibn Batuta's description, *circa* 1344, of the Muslim ruler of Beruwela, with his 500 horsemen; King Vatthini Bandara, the half-Moorish ruler of Kurunegala, who met his end in a treacherous and spectacular manner; and so on. We do know that, as time went by, Muslims of Tamil origin eventually came to dominate the community's ethnic mix. A third component of that mix was Malay, for Lanka experienced a series of Malay incursions during the

*Young temple dancers, made up and wearing fancy dress, (**left** and **above**) at a kovil in the hill country.*

A Brahmin priest in the goldsmiths' temple. He presides over the rites in the Nattu-Kottu-Chettiyar Kovil, Galle. In the kovil is the golden Skanda figure shown on page 23.

13th century, and the town of Hambantota, on the south coast, was a well-known port of call for Malay pilgrims en route to Mecca. The town's name is actually said to derive from the type of vessel in which the pilgrims sailed, thus: *sampan-tota*. This may be fancy, but the Malay communities of the south are a fact. The British in their time even managed to muster a regiment of them: it was the first Asiatic regiment to be awarded the King's Colours.

When the Portuguese arrived in the East, they found themselves in competition with the Muslim traders of the Arabian Sea. Lost mercantile opportunities, combined with long-standing religious enmities, resulted in some bloody battles. In Sri Lanka, the Muslims escaped their persecutors by fleeing into the hills, where the King of Kandy ruled and the *Parangis* could not follow. Here they became an important component of the overall social sructure. Sri Lanka at the time had no money economy; in fact, there was little trade of any sort, for despite the central authority of Kandy, few villages had much intercourse with each other. The Muslims came and supplied these villages with the few essentials they required from outside and, in doing so, helped to establish lines of communication between them. The Muslim trader, trudging from one isolated farming community to another alongside his pack-bull laden with salt, fine Indian cloth and other goods, became a familar sight all over the kingdom. Many later settled down to become paddy-farmers, giving up the itinerant existence which was the only one their ancestors had ever known. And here they stayed, adopting the ways of the new, settled life, yet holding fast to the faith that sustained them in their journeyings; the faith built upon five pillars, of which one is, itself, a journey: the long, weary trek of the *Haj*.

The Prophet was a practical man, and his advice regarding the *Haj* was practical also. Wait, he said, wait until you have finished your work in the world and all your debts are paid. Do not undertake the great pilgrimage until you can afford to. Sri Lanka's Muslims follow his advice, with the result that the majority never see Mecca at all. It costs too much.

It comes as a shock to most Sri Lankans to discover just how poor their Muslim minority really is. The popular image of them is quite different, for there are a few very rich Muslims, mostly concentrated in Colombo and on the West Coast, and these tend to be highly visible because they do not trouble to conceal either their wealth or their enjoymemnt of it. In fact, few rural Muslims have much in the way of fixed assets, for they prefer to keep their resources dangerously liquid. A distrust of banks and financial institutions run through all their dealings, a distrust born of religious sanction.

The community at large endures. The greater part of its culture is, of course, derived from the grand commonwealth of Islam, with its well-known rituals and observances. But a strong thread of Tamil custom can also be perceived to run through it, especially among the Muslims of the Eastern Province, who are said to preserve Sri Lankan Tamil folkways in their purest form. It is an unusual mixture, rich but not always harmonious, another priceless strand in the intricate web of Sri Lankan society.

According to the Dutch dictionary, a 'burgher' is someone who lives in a town. But while the majority of Sri Lanka's Burghers are indeed townsfolk, the name has a different meaning here.

Like all invaders, the Dutch never quite completed their withdrawal from the island. Some of the Hollanders stayed on to settle in the country. Their descendants are the Burghers. Less strictly speaking, there are Portuguese and British 'Burghers' also, though the latter are often called Eurasians — rather confusingly, since they are neither European nor Asian, but Anglo-Ceylonese! But whatever their origin, nearly all Burghers have certain traits in common. They speak English as a first language, adopt semi-European dress and manners, and profess one or another denomination of the Christian faith.

Perhaps there was a time, far in the past of some mythical Sri Lanka, when men and women of different races found no pleasure in one another, and the tribes never mingled. In the real world, blood calls as sweetly to strange blood as to kin, and everyone is a mongrel. When the Burgher community was still large enough to support the luxury of its own class system, skin colour (possibly thought to indicate racial purity) was one of its determining factors. As time went on, however, it became less important than lifestyle; the closer one's dress, speech and manners were to the European ideal, the better. It is fashionable to sneer at this sort of thing nowadays, but there is wisdom in it.

Those early Dutch exiles dared not let go the things of Europe, or Asia would drown them like a flood, take away everything that gave them a sense of their place in the world, and drive them to madness or death. The perils of 'going native' are real, as writers on both sides of the cultural divide have pointed out.

As time went by, the Burghers found their own niche in Ceylonese society, and the need for these precautions lessened. But by then they had already become part and parcel of the group's class structure and could not be done away with lightly.

Of course, European ways could not be adhered to strictly by everyone. They were too expensive. And so, Burgher culture became a fascinating blend of West and East. Christmas dinner in many Burgher homes is a sumptuous combination of traditional saffron rice and curries augmented by a very European meat platter. Breakfast could be *kiri-bath* one morning, bacon and eggs the next. Burgher ladies wear western dress about the house and to market, but at weddings and christenings, their saris and necklaces glitter as brilliantly as anybody else's.

The interpenetration of cultures is greatest where economic opportunities are least. Like the poor whites of the American South, the men of the (now almost extinct) Burgher community of Batticaloa attended church formally suited, hatted and barefoot.

Under British rule, Burghers served for the most part in the second rank of the civil administration. Many found employment in the postal services, the railways, the conservation service and the police. Exploration and discovery appealed to their adventurous natures, and some came to know the land better than those whose forbears had lived on it, and farmed it, for centuries. Men with names like Engelbrecht, Spittel, Keuneman and Dekker quartered the island with sketchpad, notebook and camera; they introduced Sri Lanka to her people.

With the advent of Independence came an upsurge of Ceylonese nationalism, and Sinhala replaced English as the official language. Thousands of Burgher civil servants found themselves at a terrible disadvantage, for the documents now landing on their in-trays were incomprehensible to them. To make matters worse, they often found their new superiors as incomprehensible as the documents; the feeling was reciprocated. Many were forced to retire and face the

These Jaffna almshouse-keepers proudly pose with the portrait of their founder.

strictures of life on a government pension. The second blow came when English ceased to be the traditional medium of instruction in Sri Lankan schools. To most Burghers, it seemed as if the policy-makers had forgotten them, or just did not care.

Today, the Burghers of Sri Lanka are faced with an agonizing choice. They must choose their inheritance. To put it another way: they must assimilate to the local culture, or emigrate. The choice is being forced on them by circumstances, and often the decision is, too. Opting for the Western part of their heritage calls for money, work-permits and visas, all hard to come by. Very often, those who would rather go must stay because they cannot afford to leave.

Those who do leave often find that Australia or Canada offer cold comfort. Yet they cannot return, for there is seemingly no welcome to be found at home.

There are still other peoples in Sri Lanka, even smaller in number than the vanishing Burghers. There are the Kuravar or Ahikuntakayo, the so-called 'gypsies' of Sri Lanka, who charm snakes and tell fortunes for a living, and wander from village to village by routes whose antiquity rivals *samsara* itself. They are said to have come here from India and to be related to similar folk who wander about there.

The Kaffir people of the Puttalam district came from farther abroad, but their origins are more clearly discernible; they are descended from the Bantu tribes of Africa and were brought here by the Portuguese, who used them as cannon-fodder. One of them was Chief Executioner to the last king of Kandy, the paranoid, despotic Sri Vickrama Rajasinha.

There are the Malays and 'Indian' Tamils, subsets of larger ethnic groups as far as the census-takers are concerned. Census-takers are rarely concerned with more than the forms they make us fill; both groups are as different from, as they are similar to, the larger minorities they are lumped with.

There are the Chinese. The Afghans. The Sindhis, Borahs and Parsis from North India.

One day all the diversity will be gone. One day, there will be only Sri Lankans. It is the way of countries. It will not happen tomorrow, and it will not happen without conflict, but it will happen.

But the way of countries is not the way of Nature, who abhors uniformity as much as she does a vacuum. Europe is finding that out today, as hordes of foreign invaders storm her gates seeking jobs and political refuge, and her own youth split themselves into tribes and subcultures. In Sri Lanka, the old communal divisions may blur and fade, but other lines of demarcation will appear to replace them, for better or for worse. The kaleidoscope twists, the pattern changes. The actual elements of Sri Lanka's fabulous diversity may change, but the diversity itself is unaltered. The dancing god dances on.

*People from the Kali Amman Kovil, Modera, near Colombo: temple priest (**top left**); a "mother", one of the female attendants of the goddess (**above**); a wary devotee (**bottom left**).*
***Following double page**: Swamis at mealtime prayer, Selvacchanithi Murugan Kovil, Jaffna.*

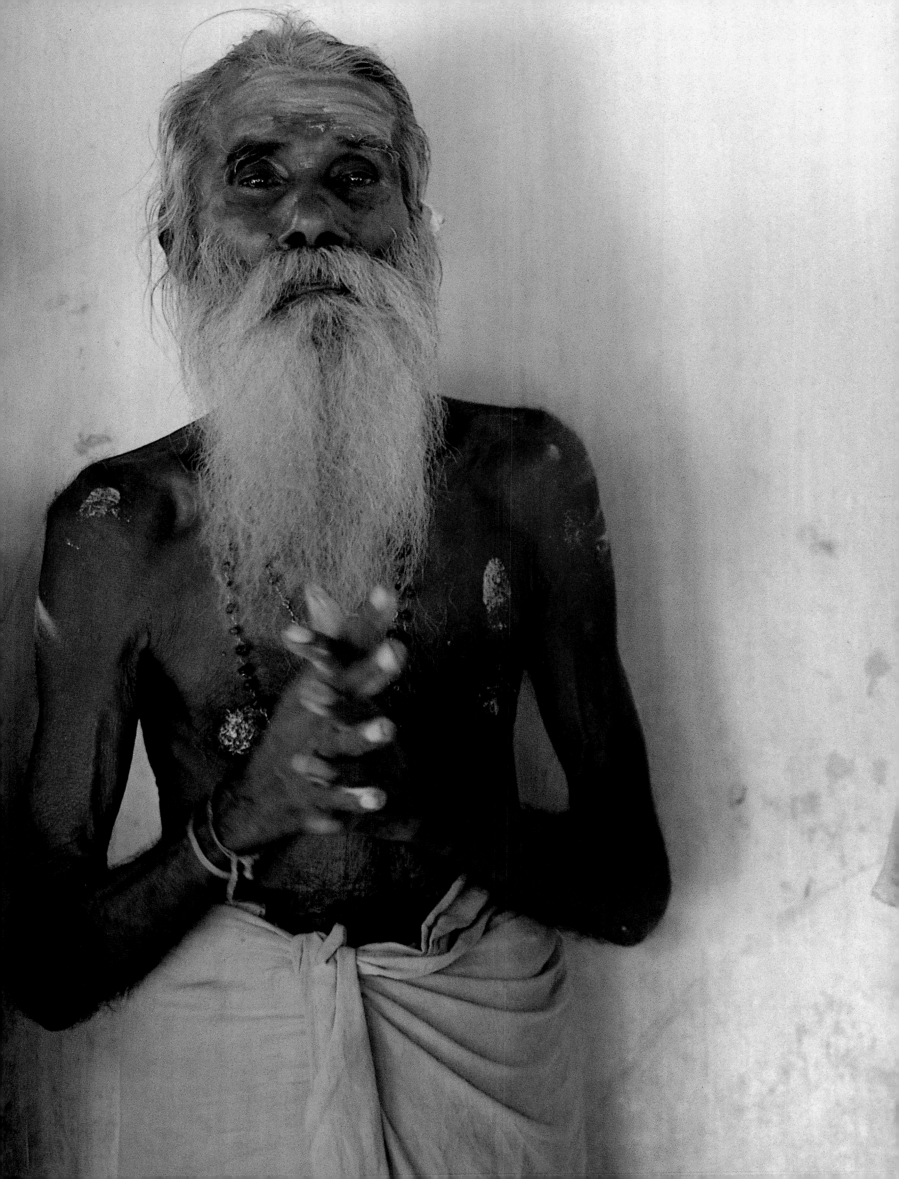

SPICE ISLAND
The culinary blowtorch

IF SRI LANKA DOES NOT HAVE THE WORLD'S most fiery cuisine, the country that does must feature natives with cast-iron insides. It is hard to imagine anything hotter than the island's hottest curries and *sambals* — so pungent they can make faces flush and eyes water — being enjoyed by mere mortals. Sri Lanka lies as far inside the Torrid Zone of gastronomy as anyone could want to go. Of course, sting on its own is not enough. Good Sri Lankan cooks know

that the chili, like all strong spices, must be handled with tact, lest its assertive personality ruin that subtle balance of flavour which makes a fine curry. There are cooks whose understanding of this balance is so profound they create perverse masterpieces: the infatuated diner eats on, powerless to resist, despite his pounding heart, the tears streaming down his cheeks and the live coal that seems to have taken up residence in his mouth.

Visitors are rarely exposed to the full blast of the culinary blowtorch. Centuries of experience have taught us to prepare our guests slowly, starting them off with milder dishes and graduating them to delights like *katta sambal* only after their palates have acquired some 'seasoning'. There is no shortage of gentler substitutes, because the cuisine of Sri Lanka is as diverse as its history and culture are. Indian, Arab, Malay, Portuguese, Dutch and Indonesian influences have all grafted themselves on to the domestic tradition and live amicably together in the Sri Lankan kitchen. The British Empire, with its boilings and steamings, is sometimes there also, but we do not boast about it.

It is proper that all these cultures should meet among the cooking-pots, for it was food that brought them to this country in the first place; more accurately, spices to preserve and enhance the flavour of food. Nutmeg, mace, cloves, pepper and, above all, cinnamon were old Serendib's most famous exports. It was said in those days that you could smell the spice-gardens several miles offshore as your ship approached the island. If our food has a reputation for being spicy, then, it is only because we have so many of the ingredients near at hand. We can afford to be prodigal. And prodigal we certainly are.

The kitchen in any Sri Lankan household would find daily, or a least weekly, use for a score of different spices and garnishes, among which feature cardamon, carraway, coriander, lemon-grass, mustard, tamarind and turmeric, in addition to those already mentioned. And of course, the ubiquitous chili is ever present: fresh, roasted or dried, in every variety from big, mild capsicums to tiny, white-hot *kocchi*. Without spices, the great Sri Lankan curry would be an impossibility.

To put it rather crudely, curry is a savoury sauce of coconut milk in which meat, fish or vegetables are cooked; there are 'dry' curries also. To make a curry, one starts with the spices. The actual combination varies with the dish being prepared and the cook's personal taste. The final combination may be lightly dry roasted, then ground together into a fine powder. Ideally, all the ingredients should be freshly-ground every time a curry is prepared. Accomplished cooks would not dream of using proprietary packaged curry powders because they know the importance of freshness and the need to vary the palette of flavours for every dish. After the spices are prepared, they, along with other flavouring ingredients, are added to the coconut milk to make the basic sauce in which the food, whether meat or vegetable, is cooked. The trick is to use spices to augment, not smother, the taste of the food. Chicken, fish, shellfish and red meat all have their separate songs, and the accompaniment must change to fit the melody. So called 'white' curries, mild and tangy, are for fish and vegetables. Darker curries have hearts of fire and set off meat best. Fish is prepared in several different ways, of which *ambul thiyal* — a hot-sour tuna preparation as black as a fiend's waistcoat — is perhaps the best loved.

Previous double page: Farmers threshing paddy at Tissamaharama. Contemporary elements in the timeless scene are strictly utilitarian. The finest curd-and-treacle shop of all Sri Lanka is hidden away in a corner of the old Galle market (left). A fishwife (above) in Negombo wears a smile and bright colours.

*The proper technique for eating with your hands is demonstrated by
this late luncher in a ricefield at Ilukkumbura, near Matale.*

Any tropical island worthy of the name must boast an abundance of shellfish, and Sri Lanka is no exception. Having tasted curried crab, one is apt to decide that there is really no other way to enjoy them. Lobster are not highly prized (too big and bland; export-market stuff), but prawns are superb curried or fried, and squid responds well to the latter treatment.

A typical Sri Lankan luncheon or dinner is a meal of rice and curry. There will be several of the latter, but meat will not predominate. Of four or five curries, only one, or perhaps two, will be meat dishes. The rest will be vegetarian. There will also be a *mellun*, a sort of finely-chopped salad, a sambal and perhaps a pickle or two. At the centre of the table, with the smaller curry dishes circling it like satellites orbiting Jupiter, is the star of the show, a great dish heaped high with rice.

Rice is the staff of life. In a culinary sense, the array of other dishes are simply flavouring, intended to make the bland white staple more attractive. The sambals in particular serve this function, for they are essentially flavour-concentrates; red-hot concoctions of chopped onions, shallots or grated coconut, their bite is further enhanced by lime-juice and tiny slivers of dried and cured tuna called "Maldive fish". With the aid of these lesser dishes and their flavours, vast amounts of rice are consumed.

But if Sri Lankan cuisine is dominated by rice and curry, it certainly does not end with it. Curry is eaten with other staples too: *hoppers* and *stringhoppers*, the latter a soft circle woven from stringy dough. The former not really describable, except inadequately as a sort of biscuit of leavened rice-flour, sometimes with an egg baked into the centre.

Hoppers hot from the pan, eaten with one hot meat curry, *seeni* sambal or *katta* sambal, and fresh fruit before or after, are the finest breakfast in the world. Pots of hot tea wash it all down. Other breakfast specialities are *pittu*, crumbling steamed cylinders of flour and grated coconut, and *kiri-bath*. The name means "milk-rice", and that is what it is, rice cooked in coconut milk that hardens into a kind of cake when it cools. *Kiri-bath* is a festive dish, associated with the *Avurudu*, or New Year, and with beginnings of all kinds.

All of the dishes and snacks previously mentioned are Sinhalese food, at least by adoption. The Tamil kitchen produces curries too, along with other delicacies, very much like the food of South India. *Thosai* or

dosa, large, flat cakes of sourdough, are popular, eaten like rice with an array of other dishes or with *sambaal*, a sort of curry containing several different kinds of vegetable. Tamil curries are generally more liquid than Sinhalese ones. Other favourites are *vadai*, small lentil-cakes or savoury doughnuts. Tamil food is usually, though not invariably, vegetarian.

Each Sri Lankan ethnic group has its own distinct cuisine, and all those passing visitors left their mark too. *Buriyani*, that old Moghul favourite, is the *pièce de résistance* of Muslim cooking. The base is rice boiled in meat stock, served with greasy, spicy meat (mutton is most authentic) and mint relish. The result is exquisitely rich, savoury and, for those who worry about such things, sinfully fattening.

In South Asian culture, Muslims are the meat specialists; in Sri Lanka, where the Buddhist faith makes most Sinhalese reluctant to take life, they have a near-monopoly on the trade. Muslim cafes in Colombo and other towns are often the only places open all night. They specialise in quick service with minimum ceremony, the Sri Lankan equivalent of Kentucky Fried Chicken. The quality of the food itself is variable; at its best, it can be excellent.

Lamprais have the same base as buriyani — rice in meat stock — although the resemblance between the two more or less ends there. The dish is apparently of Dutch East Indian origin and features a variety of curries, sambals, meatballs and other delicacies, all wrapped along with the rice in a banana leaf and baked so that the flavours mix and mingle. Unwrapping the *lamprais* from its enclosing leaf releases an aroma like the breath of the Spice Island itself.

Other Dutch treats include *broeder*, a sort of cake that only comes out at Christmas, and *kokijs*, crisp wheels of pastry cut in fanciful shapes.

Love-cake, rich, sweet and heavy, is a Burgher speciality. Burgher cooking is as cosmopolitan as the community's origins and effortlessly blends East and West together; a little of this, a pinch of that, a spoonful or so of the other. The result of these generations of experiment, transcending ethnicity, may well be the finest Sri Lankan cuisine of all.

After the main course, we come to the dessert. Despite the British influence, Sri Lankans never acquired much of a taste for the sort of sweet and creamy confections popular in the West. Here the best dessert of all is a selection of the fruits of the island. The choice is practically endless; a catalogue of the more readily available delights appears elsewhere in this book. The other traditional favourite is curds and honey. The "honey" is actually coconut treacle, and the curds (yoghurt) should be made thick and fresh, from buffalo milk. The treacle is used for topping.

The Muslims have a dessert called *wattalapam* that is as rich as the rest of their festive board. It is made from solidified coconut treacle (*hakuru*), coconut milk, eggs, nuts and spices: a sort of caramel.

Traditional Sinhalese confectionery is sweet and dark, like the confectioners themselves. It has a chewy rather than melt-in-the-mouth consistency. The sweetening agent is invariably coconut treacle, which has a flavour of its own, quite unlike plain sugar. It is therefore less versatile than sugar, for that flavour is present in all things sweetened with it.

As a result, all Sinhalese sweetmeats are of rather uniform character, and cooks create unique treats by concentrating solely on qualities of bite and texture. *Kavun, kalu dodol, halape* and *thalaguli* are among the most popular and illustrate the situation well: the first is rich and oily, the second a slightly granulated jelly, the third rather dry, with a rural character imparted to it by the *kurakkan* flour with which it is made, and the fourth hard and chewy.

Sinhalese sweetmeats have something else in common besides treacle. They are all rather difficult to prepare, requiring a lot of time and labour to obtain a palatable result. In fact, much the same could be said of Sri Lankan cooking in general, at least compared to the contemporary Western approach. Cleaning rice for the pot, grinding and roasting spices, the rough business of scraping and grating coconuts, then squeezing the gratings to yield their milk — all these things take time. In *Mediaeval Sinhalese Art*, Ananda Coomaraswamy describes how a traditional Sinhalese house was furnished. His list of kitchen-implements paints a toilsome picture:

"... a set of earthen pots, a vegetable slicer, a coconut scraper (hiramanaya), a stone for grinding curry-stuffs, a water-dipper, baskets for corn, wooden spoons, and a spoon rack were the principal requirements. Three stones, (lig-gal) formed the cooking hearth, supporting an earthen pot over a wood fire."

The picture in most rural homes is hardly different today, and food is still prepared in the old, traditional manner. There are many people who maintain that it tastes best cooked that way.

Culture shock is often felt most keenly at table, where manners and customs probably vary more from country to country than the actual food does. In Sri Lanka, people eat with their fingers.

Most patriotic Sri Lankans feel compelled to defend the ancient custom. The author will not do the same, although he himself eats with his fingers quite frequently. Where proper concern for, and understanding of, the principles of hygiene and sanitation prevail, it is a perfectly safe custom; where they do not, it can be deadly. A glance at certain UNICEF statistics proves as much, but it is no use trying to abolish the custom. And it is not even necessary: soap and water cost less than knives and forks.

The proper way to eat with one's fingers is as follows. Only the right hand is used (an ancient sanitary precaution, rendered ineffective by a simple *ayubovan*). With the fingers, one selects small pinches

An overturned jar sounds the only note of disorder in a spick-and-span ayurvedic *dispensary (**left**). Once, European apothecaries' shops must have looked rather like this. Choosing tomatoes (**above**) is serious business on a market day in a rural township.*

from the array of curries on one's plate, adds them to the rice and mixes them together lightly. One then lifts food to mouth with the fingers, using the thumb as a lever. It is not messy; not a grain need be spilled; and Sri Lankans prepare and present food in such a manner that this is really the only way to enjoy it.

It is considered bad form to get food on one's hand beyond the top two finger-joints, although the custom is less strict in Tamil households.

There are two Sri Lankan alcoholic beverages, both gifts of the bounteous coconut-palm. One is toddy, the fermented sap of the coconut flower, and the other arrack, a distillate of toddy.

Toddy is a milky brew with a strong characteristic taste; though it is not very potent, the mornings-after can be rough. Toddy-tapping is an extremely difficult process, since the coconut flower grows high off the ground. Aerial ropeways are slung between the trees, and along these the toddy-tapper walks, his pot and the mysterious implements he uses to start the sap slung about his waist. The palmyrah and *kitul* palms also produce toddies, each with a distinct flavour, bouquet and character of its own.

Arrack is serious business. Sri Lankan arrack is a true indigenous beverage and another of ancient Lanka's famous exports. It has the appearance of whisky, but tastes completely different. The alcohol content is generally between 30 and 40%, less potent than most western whiskies and rums, but strong enough to generate some very good vibrations.

Arrack is the national drink, and you will find it everywhere in Sri Lanka, except in the luxury hotels of Colombo, where few native things are thought socially acceptable. An arrack and lime might be the smoothest introduction to this Sri Lankan spirit.

No McDonald's here. No Kentucky Fried Chicken. No food franchise outlets of any type or description. Western food is available readily enough in Colombo and most populous rural areas, though in the latter it is hardly *cordon bleu*. At the dining table, as in so many other areas, Sri Lankans remain closely bound to tradition. Not all of us, all the time, are patient with this, but, on the whole, we prefer it that way. Visitors who are willing to step outside the air-conditioner's charmed circle usually find they like it too.

After all, things could be worse. In India you have to drink Indian-made coca-cola.

*Onions, small, medium and large, are featured at Trincomalee
market. Onions are important ingredients in Sri Lankan cuisine,
where vegetables are favoured over meat as the central attraction.*

Fibreglass fishing-boats turn Negombo harbour into a patchwork quilt. Despite the adoption of modern equipment, much of the rhythm of fishing life still feels traditional.

CRAFTS
The work of our hands

LONG AGO, EVEN A RELATIVELY POOR HOME was often filled with beautiful things; not ornaments, but commonplace utensils made to see hard daily use. Furniture, tableware and kitchen implements were beautiful almost by accident, because they expressed in themselves their makers' dedication to their craft. It is hard for us to imagine such a thing, for we have grown used to the ugliness of mass production, but there was once a time when no two made objects was alike, and each had a special character of its own.

However, the crafts industry was forced upmarket by the Industrial Revolution, so that today, that sort of beauty is only for the rich. At least, that is how it is in the industrialised world. In Sri Lanka, traditional hand-made objects still supply many of the rural people's needs. Many are simply poorly made, but there are still places where a tradition of fine craftsmanship lingers, and beautiful things can easily be found. And they need not always be expensive.

Mats are a good example. They are part of the furniture in every rural home, and most, nowadays, are uninteresting. But in the village of Henawela in Dumbara, there is still a clan of weavers who make hempen mats according to an ancient technique. The mats are woven with decorative motifs — stripes, geometrical designs, stylised birds — that have not changed in centuries. The Dumbara weavers are relics of a time when even mundane objects like mats and ropes were made by castes of hereditary craftsmen. The quality of their craft recalls a time when fine work was valued for itself, rather than for what it might bring on the market.

Basketware is rarely called upon to hold water, yet Jaffna basketware, woven out of palmyrah-leaf, can often do just that. Not watertight, but still serviceable and beautiful, is the basketware to be found in the Kalutara district, just south of Colombo. Sinhalese basketware can be made of rattan, bamboo, rushes or palm-leaves. Its form is unsophisticated, yet satisfying. The same can be said of the terracotta pottery of Kelaniya and the South, reddish-brown, unglazed pieces of which can be found in homes all over the country. Pottery is one of the basic Sri Lankan crafts, for clay pots, called *hutti*, are the standard cooking

utensil. A curry cooked in a clay pot over a wood fire tastes quite unlike the same thing prepared in a metal pan on a modern cooker. Every home will also boast a *kalegediya*, a pottery water-vessel whose porous walls keep the water inside deliciously cool, whatever the temperature outside, so long as the *kalegediya* itself stands in the shade.

Wooden objects are often decorated with lacquer-work called *biralu-vada*. Sri Lankan lacquer-work is a far cry from the sophisticated, highly finished intricacies of Chinese and Japanese lacquer tradition. *Biralu-vada* is lacquer decoration applied to an object spinning on a lathe. A stick of coloured lac is pressed lightly to the turning object, and the heat of friction causes it to melt and mark the wood. *Niyapothu-vada*, or 'fingernail-work', is more delicate: the heated lac is pulled out into strands which are laid on to the wood in patterns. The filament runs over the worker's fingernails, which guide it and snip it short when necessary. The lacquer is a natural product, exuded by plants whose twigs have been pierced by the lac-beetle. The colouring is added in the form of powdered pigment.

Not all Sri Lankan crafts are simple and unsophisticated. The island's forests boast a number of fine hard cabinet-woods, including teak, satinwood, mahogany, rosewood and ebony. Wood-carving, both on furniture and as a form of architectural decoration, is a Sinhalese speciality. Some of the finest examples of the latter can be found at Embekke *devale* near Kandy. The *devale* is also noteworthy for its wealth of fine Kandyan craft objects. In fact, *vihares* and *devales* are often full of exquisite objects and decoration, for, as one might expect, craftsmen expended their best efforts in the service of religion.

Previous double page: Stilt-fishermen casting in light surf, somewhere on the South Coast. Fern-leaves form a beard (left) for a Bacchus-like stone head in a garden of Bevis Bawa, at Brief, Bentota. Textures resonate with these keys to a Buddhist temple (above).

Lacquerwork is a common craft on the Subcontinent and in the Buddhist societies of Thailand and Burma. These canisters, on sale at a government handicraft centre, display the Sri Lankan style. Spot the matched pair.

Clockwise from top left: Nagaraksa *and* Guruluraksa *demons represented in exorcists' masks; fish boxes, Kocchikade; lacquer boxes in Colombo; detail of a sesath parasol; cart wheel; folk terracotta at the Hutti village fair; spices on sale, Kandy market. This carved Ravana image (**above**) is on a temple chariot in Jaffna.*

Woodcarving often took the form of low-relief work, which adorned furniture and decorative panels. There have been experiments with carving in the round, but traditional woodwork never takes this form.

Another, specialised type of wood carving is mask-making, generally confined to the South Coast. The *kolama* is Sinhalese folk drama, played by actors in masks. The masks represent stock *kolam* characters and are often quite complicated in design, with moving jaws and eyeballs. The overall effect is of caricature.

The purpose for which the best-known Sinhalese masks are designed contrasts darkly with the light-heartedness of *kolam*. The grotesque visages that so attract tourists are in fact exorcists' masks, used in the 'devil-dances' of the low country. The real masks (on which the souvenir-stand imitations are modelled) represent the actual demons and, for certain esoteric reasons, must be carved by the dancer himself. The form of the mask and the colours with which it is stained, must adhere to strict specifications if the exorcism is to go as planned.

In the kingdom of Kandy, the highest craft caste after the weavers of fine cloth (who were often of Indian descent) was the caste of artificers, or metal-workers. Sri Lankan metalworkers used most common and precious metals and their alloys, with sub-castes specialising in gold, silver and so on. Modern Sri Lankan metalwork preserves a high standard and often employs lovely traditional motifs.

Sea Street in the Pettah is the modern Goldsmiths' Quarter; each shop, usually Tamil-owned, is a miniature Alladin's Cave. Gold plays a vital role in social ritual: Sinhalese and Tamil brides will generally receive a gold necklace from their husbands, no matter how poor the latter may be. Gold jewellery is prized as a hedge against inflation and an easily portable asset.

Filigree silver jewellery, as well as pieces made from an alloy called *paslo* — "five metals" — often recall Indian work of a similar sort. Antique jewellery shops sell chains, bracelets and anklets, finger-and toe-rings, hairpins and every imaginable adornment. Again, beauty and price are not necessarily related.

Brasswork is popular, and variable in quality. Most Sinhalese and Tamil homes employ certain brass objects for religious and customary purposes — lamps, incense-holders and the like. These are usually cast. Trays, boxes and flatware are made in cutwork, the metal cut to the required pattern and then engraved if necessary. The *repoussé* technique creates raised patterns on the surface of the metal.

There are, of course, a host of other crafts — lacemaking, ivory and tortoiseshell carving, the making of *gokkola* palm leaf decorations for ceremonial occasions, and so on. It would take a scholarly monograph to do justice to them all, and one such already exists (see bibliography). It says little of lapidary, however, except to mention that gems were usually cabochon cut and not faceted.

Cabochon-cut gemstones sparkle less, but glow more subtly. Sri Lankan jewellers are rarely impressed with mere glitter, for they encounter prodigies of brilliance everyday. Until recently, the island was one of the world's two largest producers of fine coloured gemstones. Nor are her reserves near to being exhausted.

The gem-mining country of Sabaragamuwa and Elahera abounds with stories of incredible finds: the man who discovered a huge blue sapphire while digging a well, the trucker who came upon an even larger stone when he reversed his lorry into an earthen embankment. Serendipity strikes again. Geologists say most of Sri Lanka is gem-bearing soil, though the depth at which the stones are to be found varies.

Gems are mined from "pits". The soil of the pit often contains a variety of different gems: rubies, sapphires, cat's-eyes, tourmalines, all jumbled together in the *illam*, the gem-bearing gravel that lies beneath a layer of alluvial clay. The pits are an unimpressive sight, mudholes worked by men in loincloths. The miners scoop the *illam* into baskets. These are swirled about in a second pit filled with water until the mud is washed away and the gemstone, should there be one, is revealed, glowing like an eye in the earth.

If gem-mining is a messy business, gem-trading can be even more so. Yet trust between buyer and seller is vital at certain stages for, despite recent technological advances, judging the quality of a stone is still a matter of experience and instinct.

The trade in gems is centuries old on the island, though modern economists persist in calling them a "non-traditional export". In an age when "peacocks, apes and ivory" have been replaced by more prosaic goods, precious stones add a necessary exoticism—an ornament, so to speak, to the nation's trade.

It is often hard to say where craft leaves off and art begins. In an ideal world perhaps they would be not two different things, but one. It is beyond our scope to examine that evidence or to adduce reasons for the split. One cause may have been consciousness of self; the craftsman wakes up one day with a sense of the expressive power of his hands and becomes an artist.

The world of the hereditary craftsman was, in a sense, Edenic. He did not choose his trade; the choice was made for him by the inflexible laws of caste. Apprenticed to one who stood in relationship to him as parent and even deity, he absorbed craft skills by the process of precept, rote and observation. By the time he came to set up on his own, he would not so much possess his craft as be possessed by it. The monotony of workshop routine, the endless practice, the reverence paid both lore and master, all would combine to create a unity of craft and craftsman. Unlike the artist, whose skill is only a means to his art, the craftsman was incapable of producing anything else. He would have no need for ambition, for such things are only cheap substitutes for the thing he possessed: the knowledge that fine work is not a living, but life itself.

*Brass coconut-oil lamps like this one from a Buddhist temple (**left**), are lit as part of the ceremony to mark the Sinhalese New Year or the inauguration of a new entreprise. A brass tray (**above**) bears the tools that shaped it. Note the huge iron dividers.*

Clockwise from top left: Coconut trees; gokkola flower decorations; palmyrah fence; gokkola trompe-l'oeil; young palms; rush-mat weave; dyed coconuts; young palm leaves. Gokkola decorations (*above*) adorn the poruwah at Sinhalese weddings. *Following double page*: Lotus-blossoms and smiles at Kataragama.

ATTITUDES
Chaos and rules

THEY SAY TWO ENGLISHMEN STANDING AT a bus-stop will instinctively form a queue. One hundred and thirty-three years of British rule were not enough to inculcate the same habit into the Ceylonese, however. We form queues only with the greatest reluctance and jump them with alacrity the minute authority turns its back. The bus service employs marshals to control the mob at crowded bus-stands, harrassed men about whom futility hangs like a

cloud. They share their penance with cinema clerks, army drill sergeants and point-duty policemen. Sri Lankans dislike being regimented. Visitors to Colombo are often disturbed by the apparent chaos they see around them. Everyone seems intent on his or her purpose and never mind the rest. Collisions are frequent, arguments vociferous. A visitor is apprehensive: he has a dinner invitation tonight; if Sri Lankans are so unruly in public, how do they conduct themselves in the privacy of their homes?

He keeps the invitation, and is astonished. The hospitality he experiences may be grave and ceremonious or easy and informal, but whichever it is, it will be graceful and stamped with a genuine concern for his well-being. He no longer fears that he has come among barbarians; in fact, as dinner progresses, he begins to suspect that the opposite has happened. From wondering at the deftness with which his host and hostess anticipate his wants, he comes to realise that a like sensitivity is expected of him. Lapses in manners will be acknowledged only by the subtlest of signs. If perceptive, he may even catch a glimpse of the web of practice and custom, fine and strong like a spider's, that underlies every casual action or word.

At this point, bewilderment sets in. Can these really be the same people who drive like maniacs, fart inconsiderately in crowded places and hold riotous parties in quiet neighbourhoods until dawn? What is going on here? How to resolve the contradiction between the public and the private faces?

In fact, what looks like anarchy is nothing of the sort. If we Sri Lankans are free and uninhibited in our public expressions, it does not mean that we are a society without rules. On the contrary, close inspection reveals that, especially in the villages, all

activity follows a pattern that has changed very little in centuries. We follow it naturally, without thinking, so that casual observers sometimes conclude that we are doing just as we please. And in a sense, we are.

But the pattern that governs our lives does not concern itself with road manners or bazaar etiquette. Society restrains and restricts us in the larger aspects of our lives, so we must compensate by expressing our individuality in every little way we can.

And if we place a high premium on individual expression, perhaps it is because we are such a mixed bunch. The country's people are said to be made up of four main ethnic groups, but a short walk down Chatham Street at rush-hour will make nonsense of this bureaucratic fiction; here are a dozen or more identifiable racial influences, and their admixture has created an incredible variety of face and form. "Ceylon is the cradle of the human race because everyone there looks an original," said George Bernard Shaw, who ought to have known, being a noteworthy original himself. In spite of the homogenizing effect of custom and tradition, that originality remains. Zoning boards, Bauhaus functionalism and pinstriped suits are heresy in Sri Lanka; even photocopiers break down with uncanny regularity in the humid climate.

There is a Sri Lankan national character, about which much has been written: gentle yet combative, friendly, hospitable, argumentative, and so on. In dealing with individual Sri Lankans, visitors report that these attributes do, indeed, recur. Yet some also complain bitterly that you cannot count on any particular one being there when you need it. Sri Lankans, of course, take gleeful delight in this inconsistency. Among us, only originality is guaranteed.

Mara Yakka, the Demon of Death (**above**). *A southern dancer like this one must carve his own mask if it is to be ritually effective as a means of exorcising demons. The music for these dancers is provided by drummers like this one (**left**).*

*Kataragama: A bare-chested penitent performs preliminary rites before "taking the kavadi" (**right**). **In the foreground above**, the "Kavadi Master" with a saucer of burning camphor. The kavadi is carried by devotees at the Kataragama festival.*

*Young Sinhalese boys may spend a year or two as Buddhist novices,
returning to the laity when they grow older. In the old days, this
was often their only route to an education.*

This nun or bikkhuni *brings an offering of food at the temple of the sacred Bo tree, Anuradhapura. While women are far less likely to don the robes than men, a sizeable female order exists.*

*Kuravar mother and child (**above**), and young men (**right**). The Kuravars, snakecharmers by occupation, are Sri Lanka's very own "Gypsies". They are related to similar tribes in South India.*

*Known to his friends as "the last of the great White Hunters", Mike Northway (**above**) is in fact an ardent conservationist and by no means in as uneasy a confrontation with Sri Lankan culture as this juxtaposition may suggest. **At right**, a Kataragama penitent.*

These Southern dancers (**above**) array themselves in polychrome
finery, the glitter and mirrors on their costumes shining in the
firelight of a night performance. These dancers are from
Ambalangoda, and the mask of the one in the Nagaraksa
costume (**right**) is from the Ambalangoda Mask Museum.

*These women (**left**) holding their children in their arms hope that
the future holds better days for the next generation.
Above: Matara Swami at Kataragama.*

WHEN YOU CHANGE TRAINS, MIND YOU DON'T lose your luggage. Sri Lanka almost did, when she hopped aboard the westbound Progress Express at the start of the Twentieth Century. Some of her bags are, in fact, still missing, but most have been recovered. Among the latter is the indigenous artistic tradition. Credit for its revival belongs, in large measure, to the '43 Group. The riches of our country's past meant little to educated Ceylonese in the

first half of the century. Indigenous culture was not much appreciated, despite the exhortations of Coomaraswamy, Winzer and the like; instead, the prevalent taste was for western art of the most unadventurous Victorian type. The Ceylon Society of Arts, formed at the turn of the century to cultivate "the artistic instinct in the Ceylonese", was the official champion of this attitude, and the earliest Sri Lankan artists (in the western sense of the term) were associated with it: Gate Mudaliyar Tudor Rajapakse, David Paynter and Mudaliyar A C G S Amarasekara. The last named, possibly the most eminent, was to fight a bitter rearguard against the influence of Modernism in the pages of the 'Ceylon Daily News' during the late '30s. It was a sorry postscript to a distinguished career.

The '43 Group blew a hurricane of fresh air through the over-upholstered Victorian nursery. Formed under the aegis of Mudaliyar Amarasekara's chief opponent, the well-known pianist and photographer Lionel Wendt, it brought together the individual talents of a band of Sri Lankan artists who were influenced by new developments in western art as well as by ancient Sri Lankan traditions. The exploration of indigenous art traditions was willed, self-conscious and often rather uncomfortable, but it was a step in the right direction. In spite of public vilification, the group maintained its cohesion (and its productivity) until 1964, when the final Group exhibition was held.

Of the three artists featured on these pages, only the late L T P Manjusri was actually a member of the '43 Group. Brilliant artist, Manjusri was also a connoisseur of experience, and it turned his life into a long adventure, annotated by his paintings. Born in 1902 to a poor fishing family, his first creative experience was as a car-

penter's apprentice. He ran away from home while still a boy and became a *bikkhu* at the age of 13. His scholastic work began with the translation of several Bengali works into Sinhala, and from 1932 to 1934, he studied Sanskrit, Chinese and Japanese at Shantiniketan, Rabindranath Tagore's academy in India. It was here that he began painting for the first time. He travelled to Tibet to study Tantric art and returned to Sri Lanka in the 1940s. After a brief period of incarceration as a suspected Japanese spy (no one could understand his wandering, sketchbook in hand, through the southern jungles), Manjusri gave up scholarship for art and put aside his *bikkhu*'s robes. Exhibiting with the '43 group, and on his own in Europe, his career as an artist lasted until shortly before his death in 1982.

Donald Friend was an Australian who came to Sri Lanka from Bali and lived and worked here for some years; Barbara Sansoni is a Sri Lankan, perhaps best known for her architectural drawings and the use of colour in her handwoven textile designs. Her active career, like that of Laki Senanayake, an architect, painter, sculptor and maker of fine botanical studies whose palm-frond chandelier for the Main Chamber of Parliament is shown on page 220, is of somewhat more recent origin and continues today.

Each artist's work is a personal statement, not to be confused with another's, yet they all bear an identifiable Sri Lankan sensibility, connecting them in some way with the riches of the past. The re-establishment of this link with tradition, vital for Sri Lankan artists, was the greatest achievement of the '43 Group, for without it, the passengers on the Progress Express would not know where they have come from, or even — strange as it may seem — where they are going.

Previous double page: This painting at Subhodrarama temple, Dehiwela, represents the daughters of Death, tempting Prince Siddharta as he meditates. *Left*: Siva Chandrasekhar, by L T P Manjusri (1902-1982). From the collection of Koshika Sandrasagara. *Above*: Lady in a Hat, by L T P Manjusri. From the collection of Barbara Sansoni.

Boy and Coconut Palm, *by Donald Friend.*

Sigiriya, by Barbara Sansoni (detail). Artist's collection.

ART
The mirror of eternity

WHAT IS THE MEANING OF THE MONA LISA'S smile? The question is possibly Western art's best-loved enigma. It has produced reams of speculation, some scholarly and respectable, and some, like the work of the Japanese physician who traced the origins of the mysterious smile to a rare gastric disorder, merely amusing. Even people who know Leonardo's masterpiece only as a kitchen-calendar reproduction are aware of the issue and take sides

in it. Guessing what lies behind the expressions on painted and sculpted faces is a pleasant game.

It is also a sentimental one, and art critics tend to frown on it. However, they cannot deny that European and American art, from Goya to Grant Woods, is full of opportunities for its playing. Fine Hindu and Buddhist art, on the other hand, is not.

The dance of Siva Nataraja, the dance of Creation, is full of beauty and terror; yet on the face of the dancing god, the ancient sculptors carved no trace of expression. Nor are the countless Buddha images that stud the island any more unbending. The features of a sage in meditation

might reasonably be expected to show no feeling, but what about the thousands of representations of the Buddha in the act of discourse or of blessing? To the sentimentalist, these images are scarcely art at all.

Yet it would take a very insensitive person, and a very brave one, to stand before the Gal Vihare colossi and deny their value as art. The grouped figures, standing, seated and reclining, are too powerful for that. Instead, one comes to realise that another set of rules is at work here, a formal discipline so rigid that, by comparison, Western artists have always been as free as the air. Within those boundaries of convention, it was impossible, or at least very difficult, to improvise or originate. Personal expression was completely forbidden. The last thing an artist was supposed to do was to show himself in his work.

The reason for this is that the great art of India and Sri Lanka was invariably religious, and each work was intended to convey, with exactness and without comment, a body of ancient and complex philosophy. The individual artist was simply the conduit down which these ideas passed, and his work was the expression

of them. Nowhere in the equation was there room for his own personality.

Instead, the artist's training gave him the key to an enormous treasure-house of symbols. The intricate detail that characterises Oriental art is not merely decorative: every prop and ornament, every gesture and attitude of body has a definite symbolic value. For example, the hands of a Buddha image can assume a variety of poses, or *mudras*, each with its own specific meaning. It was only by means of such symbols that the message of the work was conveyed.

Without delving too deeply into metaphysics, this is perhaps the best way to explain why images of the Buddha and of the countless Hindu gods and godlings that encrust the temples of South India and Sri Lanka, are usually so expressionless. Facial expression would only cloud the meaning that each image conveys so precisely. There is no need to play guessing games, for everything is perfectly clear.

Of course, this explanaton will not satisfy everybody. What about the subtleties of emotion, the endless labyrinths of the human heart? Is there no place for Man in this cold cosmos of the intellect? It looks as if we have to dip into metaphysics after all.

In fact, the system accommodates man very well; it accommodates everything. The erotic sculptures of Konarak in India are well known, but ancient Sri Lankan art does not lack images of sensual love, either. The emotions, however, are another matter. Both Buddhist and the most advanced Hindu thought condemn the world of appearances as an illusion, masking the reality beyond. It is attachment to the illusion that keeps the soul bound to the endless cycle of death and rebirth; emotion is simply the expression of this attachment. According to the *Bhagavad Gita*,

Previous double page: A reproduction of the footprint at Adam's Peak, this stucco work is in the Subhodrarama temple in Dehiwela. The fresco (**left**) is from the same temple, as is the detail (**above**).

the liberated Self "rejoices not, grieves not, desires not." In an art that attempts to depict, through symbol and metaphor, the reality hidden behind the veil of *maya*, emotion, quite literally, obscures the point.

In Sri Lanka, as in Thailand, one encounters Buddha-images so often that it is very easy to forget that the figure they represent was a man, not a god, and is never worshipped in the conventional sense. This is especially hard to remember when watching devout Buddhists laying offerings of jessamine and frangipani at the feet of a huge statue. The offering is usually accompanied by a kowtow, hands clasped; surely the picture is of a supplicant kneeling before his god?

However, this is only an appearance, and we have already seen just how much value Buddhists place on appearances. In fact, the Buddha image represents a transcendent reality as much as it does a physical man, and to ensure that the representation remained exact, the artist referred to a document called the *Sariputra.*

To get some idea of how closely tradition confined those ancient artists, a glance at the *Sariputra* will do. The Sanskrit original was written around the 5th century AD by the man whose name it bears, and translated into Sinhalese some 700 years later. In it, the rules according to which images of men, gods and the Buddha were fashioned are laid down. There is a separate set of instructions for making standing, seated and reclining Buddha-images. Each of these is described minutely; proportionate measurements are given, not just for grosser relationships such as head-to-body, but for each limb, facial feature and even such tiny details as the eyelids, the nostrils, and the individual tufts of hair on the head (of which there must be a prescribed number: 360). Images could only be made from certain materials.

Very few artists, anywhere in the world, would accept such strictures nowadays. The *Sariputra* is not very long, yet even reading it is daunting; the mind quails at the thought of actually setting out to produce an image that accords with it. Surely the frail sprite of creativity would be crushed beneath that terrible mass of detail, like a butterfly beneath a statute-book?

Yet if this were true, all such images would look the same. They do not. Somewhere, in the cracks, individual talent shows. Some scholars argue that the *Sariputra*, and books like it, do not inhibit the great artist; they simply serve to prevent the mediocre craftsman from turning out slipshod work. This is a highly debatable viewpoint, but it is certainly true that the *Sariputra* fiercely discourages shoddiness. The text describes a variety of misfortunes that visit careless or dishonest craftsmen. A maker of hollow gold images shall suffer the loss of wife and wealth, while he who uses a crooked plumb-line shall surely be afflicted with illness. Well-placed joints will lengthen the artist's life, while poorly-placed ones could kill him.

Sariputra, the author, was not casting spells. He was simply pointing out what were, to him, the inevitable results of mishandling the construction of a precision instrument. The Buddha image was, in a sense, a lens through which the beauty and symmetry of the dhamma might be observed, and distorting the lens had consequences that would, by the law of karma, eventually cause injury to the maker.

Actually, Sariputra himself was only transcribing a far more ancient oral discipline. According to tradition, the specifications of the Buddha-image go back to the original himself. The story goes that a king sent a group of artists to attend upon the Buddha and capture his likeness. The painters tried, but were unable to do so. Finally the Enlightened One himself came to their aid. Reproving them for their poor efforts, he took a cloth and miraculously impressed his own features on it.

Stories like this one imply that the Sariputra "blueprint" produces Buddha images that are really a copy from life. This is not very likely, since no verbal

specification can ever be quite perfect and the famous cloth, which might have settled the argument, has unfortunately not been preserved.

It hardly matters. The images derived from the Sariputra need not be photographically accurate to serve their purpose. It is, as always, the inward reality that counts: the depiction of a being who is "unfettered, quiescent and absolutely pure of mind."

Like the Buddha images, the great stupas of Anuradhapura and Polonnaruwa are attempts to symbolise a reality beyond the veil of appearances. But where the former are based on an original who once existed, the latter depict an object that is entirely mythical.

Mount Meru, the mystical mountain at the centre of the cosmos, has already been mentioned in connection with the rock fortress of Sigiriya. The mountain figures in Hindu creation-myths and so became a part of Buddhist cosmology. Somewhere along the way, the legend merged with the primitive concept of the burial-mound, and out of this marriage, the stupa was born.

In the most literal sense, every stupa (or to use the term more common in Sri Lanka, *dagoba*) is indeed a burial-mound, or at least a memorial. Hidden inside the earliest dagobas are relics of the Buddha — bones, utensils and the like. However, that is by no means all. The inner chambers of the dagoba are said to also contain a model of the universe, complete with representations of the Ocean, the four continents, the god-peopled Heavens and all the rest. At the centre of the

model is the great mountain itself, with the relic-casket reposing on top. The dagoba's spire is the axis of the universe. The rings that surround the spire represent parasols, an ancient symbol of royalty, appropriate enough for the Buddha, the Lord of the Worlds.

Every Buddhist temple has its dagoba, usually of modest size. The monsters of the ruined cities contain smaller, more primitive ones at their core. These giants are unique; nowhere else in the world do stupas grow so large. The monarch of them all is the Jetavanarama dagoba, built by King Mahasena (276-303 AD). The Great Pyramid of Cheops is only slightly larger.

Within the premises of many Buddhist temples, you will find a shrine dedicated to a Hindu god. The Buddhist monks do not officiate there, but worshippers come all the same. Obviously, mankind needs deities, and the asceticism of Buddhism, while sufficient for the intellect, does not serve this more basic need.

Hinduism and Buddhism are very different. They are also very similar, and nowhere is this paradox more apparent than in their art. What, at first glance, could differ more from the serene purity of the Buddha-image, than the frozen torrent of carved shapes, motionless but uncannily alive, that makes a first visit to a Jaffna *kovil* such a disturbing experience? Yet both share a common artistic heritage and a common intent: to depict immortal truth in an impermanent figure. Western art is said to hold a mirror up to life. Indian and Sri Lankan art holds one up to eternity.

*Superb naga guardstone (**left**) at the entrance to the Ratnapasada monastery, part of the Abagiri complex at Anuradhapura. Note the seven-headed cobra hood shading the guardian's head. The feet (**above**) of the standing Buddha at Lankatilaka image-house, Polonnaruwa.*

Views at the famous vihare at Aukana: the repose of stone (**above top**) and frangipani flower offerings at the Master's feet (**above**). The 39-foot standing image of the Buddha is 1,500 years old. The brick canopy (**right**) is a modern and widely detested addition; however it does serve to protect the image.

PLEASE DON
BITTE NICHT
NE PES MON

COLOUR AND DETAIL
Dancers and drummers

THE MUSIC OF DRUMS IS THE ONLY AUTHENtic Sinhalese music. The only dancers are men and harlots. So the purists will have it. There may have been other musics once, styles in which melody and harmony had real importance; if there were, they have long since died out. In the forms of music that have survived to this day, these two elements play a minor part, or indeed no part at all. Instead, the emphasis is on rhythm and phrasing. Concentrating on these, Sinhalese musicians have developed them to incredible heights of sophistication. There are dozens of different *pades,* or rhythmic patterns, that the Sinhalese drummer must learn by heart. Virtuoso performers execute these with rapid-fire artistry, building complex cross-rhythms and improvisatory flourishes without ever missing a single beat.

The bodies that step, sway and leap in the Kandy Perahera, the weeklong Kohomba Kankariya ritual and the exorcistic dances of the Low Country, are always male. Traditionally, the Sinhalese consider it improper for a women to dance or act before an audience. Sinhalese dancing is therefore vigorous, acrobatic and exhausting. As with music, the form of the dance has taken shape according to the limitations set on it.

It has not always been so. Sinhalese royalty favoured Indian styles of music and dance, where women often performed. Leelavati, Parakramabahu's queen, was a celebrated dancer; it may have been her influence that caused the king to establish a famous academy of music and dance, the Sarasvati Mandapa, named after the Hindu goddess of music. But what is fit for kings does not always find favour with the common people who remain bound to the tradition that only one sex dances. When women must be portrayed in folk dance and folk theatre, it is always dressed-up men, not real women, who act the part.

Ancient sources name over 50 sorts of Sinhalese drum, but over the centuries, the number has dwindled to seven. Augmented by tiny cymbals and a conch-shell or *horaneva* horn fanfare on ceremonial occasions, they form the total Sinhalese ensemble.

The mainstay of the Kandyan dance is the *gete bera,* a double-headed drum measuring about 60 cm in length. The broader head is made of oxhide, the narrower, shrillersounding one of cured monkey-skin. It is played with both hands; a righthanded drummer would carry the *gete bera* with the monkey-skin to his right, for this is the "melody" head. The left hand keeps the rhythm. An energetic *gete bera* artist can make the instrument whisper or shout. Often it is possible to recognise a particular *pade* from miles away.

The sound of the *gete bera* has mystical and ritualistic associations which may predate Buddhism. So does its low-country counterpart, the *yak bera.* The name means "devildrum"; the *yak bera* is heard at exorcisms. It is a heavy, dark-coloured, double-headed cylinder meant, like its Kandyan cousin, to be played bare-handed. It produces a deep, ominous note, perfectly in keeping with its name.

The *davula* is a tubby-looking drum with two broad heads made of deer-hide. It is played with one stick and one bare hand and produces a tone which rather resembles a Western tenor drum. In fact, drums like the *davula* are found in many parts of the world, and even its name (varied according to local pronunciation) is wide-spread. In old Sri Lanka, the *davula* was the crier's drum, beaten to draw the people's attention to news and royal proclamations; its sound was also heard at state functions. Skilful players were rewarded with the gift of an ebony or ivory drumstick, chased with silver or gold. The competition for such prizes was stiff, and *davula* contests between master drummers were often prolonged until one or other of the contestants literally died of exhaustion.

Last of the four 'classical' Sri Lankan drums is the *tammettama,* a small double kettle-drum. It is played with ringed cane strikers, producing a rather dry tone.

Previous double page: Gete bera *players sounding the rhythm to which the Kandy Perahera procession marches. The Nawam Perahera, Colombo,* (**left**) *is more recent;* ginikeli, *or "fireplay", is one of the most spectacular perahera sights. A Kandyan dancer (**above**) wears the* ves, *a headdress which gleams like gold in the torchlight.*

Often mistaken by tourists for the Indian *tabla*, which it resembles, the *tammettama* is a different drum.

The remaining three Sinhalese drums are the *maddala*, sometimes called the *demala bera* or Tamil drum, the *udekkiya*, a wasp-waisted hand drum which can be returned in performance by pulling on the thong about its middle, and the *raban*. The last is a rather crude instrument with a single, nailed head. *Raban* range in size from the huge four-foot-wide monsters played at Sinhalese New Year to the tiny *virudu raban* which are balanced spinning on the ends of sticks by dancers in the Kandy Perahera. Tuning a *raban* presents rather a problem, since the head is nailed down; it can only be done by heating, and large *raban* are often played with a pot of coals beneath them to keep the drumhead taut.

Drumming and dancing are hereditary occupations in Sri Lanka; the *beravayo*, or drummer caste, monopolise the classical forms of both arts. As with all other hereditary crafts, instruction is handed down from father to son by word of mouth. Nothing, beyond a few *pade* mnemonics, is written down.

Although Sri Lankan dance bears little resemblance to contemporary Indian styles, the terms coined by Bharata, the great Sanskrit sage, are often used to describe its forms. In his famous treatise, Bharata divided dance into three main categories: *nrtta* or abstract dance, *nrtya* or expressive dance, and *natya*, drama. Sinhalese dance falls mostly into the first category, *nrtta*, in the latter's *tandava* or energetic, masculine form.

So much for jargon. All the interested layman really needs to know is that there are two main schools of Sinhalese dance, the up-country or Kandyan dance and the low-country or devil dances, so-called because their only traditional theatre of performance is the ritual exorcism. In fact, both forms have their origin in pagan magical rites, but the Kandyan dance has become highly secularised in this century, and Kandyan dancers are frequently called out on state and other public occasions.

The Kandyan dance is familiar to most Sri Lankans from the Kandy Perahera, the week-long festival in which the Tooth Relic of the Buddha is carried in solemn procession through the streets of the hill capital. The ranks of dancers in full regalia are quite capable of upstaging the elephants who walk among

them. The elephants have the advantage in size and magnificence of attire; the dancers have only their skill, but it is more than enough.

A finished Kandyan dancer is the product of a demanding apprenticeship that can go on for twenty years. Even basic movements (there are barre and off-the-barre exercises, just as in Western dance) are tricky. Once the pupil has gained a certain fluency, he is called a *naivadi* or 'undergraduate' dancer and is permitted to make limited public appearances. Before he can wear the coveted *ves*, the headdress of the finished dancer, he must dance his "finals": a performance of the Kohomba Kankariya.

The *kankariya* is a week-long invocation of the Kohomba (*margosa* tree) god. The ritual dates back to the fifth century BC and is said to exhibit the entire vocabulary of Kandyan dance. The rites begin at dusk each day and continue until sunrise. It is not a continuous performance, but a series of disjointed episodes; dancing predominates. More than fifty dancers perform, and the senior one acts as *yakdessa* or shaman, a sort of occult master of ceremonies.

Another style of Kandyan dance is the *vannam*, a repertoire of semi-expressive dances with animal themes. Here the dance begins with a thematic statement and progresses on to more abstract movements, growing more energetic and acrobatic all the time. The climatic movement is a veritable rhapsody of leaps and turns, pure body poetry.

*The splendour of the Kandy Perahera. The elephants walk among the marchers and dancers (**left**) without a collision, and negotiate the Dalada Maligawa steps with the grace of ballerinas. A Kandyan master dancer (**above**) wears the ves, reserved for dancers who share his level of skill.*

The Kandyan dancer wears the *ves*. The low-country dancer puts on a mask, representing the demon whose character he takes on in the *thovil*, or exorcism, ceremony. These ceremonies are highly theatrical. The stage is an open arena whose layout follows a prescribed occult design. A temporary "altar" acts as a backdrop. The "stage" is lit by coconut flares and reverberates to the sound of the *yak bera*. The devil-priest, or *kattadiya*, presides.

According to Sinhalese folk belief, disease is caused by demons who enter the body of the sufferer and cause his affliction. To effect a cure, the demon must be persuaded to accept an animal victim in place of his human one; and this is what the *kattadiya* tries to achieve in the *thovil* ceremony. The proceedings begin with an invitation to the demon. Then one by one, the actor-dancers who play the various demons appear. Each wears a different mask. The masks are intricately carved and vividly coloured; in the firelight, they look authentically horrifying. As the drums and incense take hold, the dancing grows more and more frenzied. The *kattadiya* addresses the prancing demons familiarly, pleading on the sufferer's behalf. Entreaties are followed by threats, and at last the offending demon (who speaks through the victim's mouth) is persuaded to accept an alternative sacrifice, usually a rooster. Sometimes the bird is killed, but more often a few drops of blood from its punctured comb suffice to placate the evil spirit.

The ceremony ends with the dispersal of various offerings at a three-way crossroads or any other significant site. As for the efficacy of the cure, it is difficult to judge, for the sufferer may be taking other forms of treatment too. The psychological effect of the ritual probably aids recovery. But whether they serve their main function or not, *thovil* ceremonies are superb, compelling theatre.

Just as there are two styles of Sinhalese dance, so are there two surviving varieties of folk theatre.

The *kolam* tradition is performed in the south of Sri Lanka. The two main centres are Ambalangoda and Mirissa. A performance can go on all night, combining dance, drama and broad comic dialogue. The actors portray stock characters and all are masked. The plays are skits on rural life, or dramatizations of popular *Jataka* stories. There is a large dollop of social satire in most *kolam* plays, mostly inoffensive jokes at the expense of bureaucrats and the upper classes. However, time has blunted some of the humour, for many *kolam* characters are colonial-period figures who have long since disappeared from the Sri Lankan scene, and their antics, though still amusing, lack the pungency they must once have had.

There are many *kolam* plots; *sokari* has just one. A Bengali couple, Sokari and Guru Hami, take ship for Lanka, where Sokari means to beg the god Kataragama to relieve her of her barren state. They are accompanied by their resourceful, cunning manservant.

Landing on the island, they encounter language difficulties (which make for some very amusing dialogue). Sokari, whose morals are not of the finest, elopes with the village apothecary. Guru Hami finds her with the help of the local Hindu priest. After he thrashes her soundly, the couple are reconciled, and soon Sokari bears a son.

Sokari performances are connected with the cult of the goddess Pattini, and each one begins and ends with an invocation to her. The play was originally staged on threshing-floors, though now any large open space will do. The performers, even Sokari herself, are all male. The action continues for seven nights, dusk to dawn. A sokari performance is a festive occasion for the villagers, who call a holiday for the duration of the proceedings.

Other traditional dance and drama styles exist. The nadagam theatre evolved from Catholic liturgical drama, but has now almost disappeared. Folk dances, performed, are also very rare except where preserved by cultural bodies. Fortunately, these vanishing forms have left their mark on contemporary dance and drama, and so will never truly die.

The best example of this is the work of Professor Ediriweera Sarathchandra, who is also known for his novels in English. His plays, Maname and Sinhabahu, are adaptations of the nadagam style to the serious modern stage. The first is a retelling of the popular Maname Jataka, the second an interpretation of the Sinhalese ancestral myth. Their appearance on the Sri Lankan scene (several decades ago, now) gave life and direction to a Sinhalese theatre that sorely needed an infusion of both qualities.

After Sarathchandra, Sinhalese theatre evolved into two distinct branches. One is concerned, as he is, with the adaptation of traditional styles to modern situations; the other, perhaps more forward-looking, takes the conventions of Western theatre and applies them to the Sinhala stage.

In the area of dance, too, traditional forms have adopted modern conventions of performance with spectacular success. The Chitrasena ballet is perhaps the most completely realised of all these efforts. There was no such thing as a Sinhala ballet until Chitrasena wrote Vidura in 1945. In the works that followed, modern choreography blended seamlessly with traditional dance forms, and a lot of idols got shattered; first (and, one hopes, least lamented), the ancient rule that reserved dancing for men only.

Chitrasena's work is a milestone in Sri Lankan art, but a successor to the tradition is sorely needed. The master himself is not growing any younger. Unfortunately, the few new choreographers currently at work do no more than feebly imitate Western styles, or so it seems, presumably under the misapprehension that carbon copies qualify as art. Tragically, the same delusion prevails in many other aspects of present-day Sri Lankan culture.

*The ceremonial ves signifies that these Kandyan dancers (**left**) have passed the test of the Kohomba Kankariya, which demonstrates their mastery of the classical repertoire. The headdress of the torchbearers at the Nawam Perahera (**above**) prevents facial blisters.*
***Following double page**: Young dancers "backstage" in Kandy.*

191

FESTIVALS
Life's re-creation

YET ANOTHER ASPECT OF THE MUCH-discussed Sri Lankan character is our capacity for having fun. When we celebrate, we do so with vigour, and often we do not stop for a week. And since, whatever the time or season, one or another of the island's many faiths and peoples will be celebrating a festival of some sort, the sight of us on holiday is one the visitor can catch at almost any time of year. The number of public holidays in the national

calendar is simply scandalous: in 1988, there were 27, not counting weekends and special Bank Holidays.

Yet gaiety is only a small part of what makes Sri Lankan festivals so spectacular. We keep solemn festival too, and these are no less absorbing. In fact, absorption is more to the point than simple enjoyment; those who participate in the festivities involve themselves completely, unconscious of self or effort. The watcher cannot help but see that these people are performing acts of real or personal significance, not going through the thing for form's or money's sake.

Yet there is no denying the pleasure of the celebration. Out come the crowds, dressed in their best, which, for the women at least, means their brightest. The pavement hawkers, who normally shut up shop once the rush-hour is over, redouble their efforts. Trays of fluorescent plastic geegaws occupy half the sidewalk, so that the mass of people is forced onto the street, to compete for space with the jammed traffic and the madcap cyclists. The scene is bright with the glow of pirated electricity. From each booth, the blare of its proprietor's favourite music issues. Horns honk. Upraised voices sound every note on the scale of urgent emotion. Over it all, amplified, distorted voices squawk relentlessly, like barkers at a carnival of lunatics.

The confusion is only peripheral, however. At its centre, there is always a sanctuary where order prevails, although the contrast with the surrounding chaos might not always be apparent to the untrained eye. This sanctuary, of course, is the area where the actual ceremonies are taking place. Whatever the festival, the events which occur within this enclosure always follow a venerable and carefully-regulated pattern. Even at the Kataragama festival, where ecstatic devotees will

sometimes appear to lose control of themselves entirely, the pattern remains, unbroken beneath the wild-eyed raptures of self-mortification, holding in check the awesome psychic forces at play among the bodies leaping in the dust.

Of course, not all Sri Lankan festivals are so abandoned in character. Some, by contrast, are marked by a lovely serenity. Of these, the most famous of all is Vesak.

Vesak falls at the May full moon. The premier festival of the Buddhist calendar, celebrated by devotees all over the world, it commemorates the birth, enlightenment and passing onward of the Buddha. It is characteristic of this austere faith that a single day suffices to celebrate the three most important events in the life of its founder; it is as if Christians had decided to celebrate Christmas, Good Friday and Easter all at once, on the same day.

The rites of Vesak are simple. People rise early, bathe and dress in white. They will then "take *sil*" at the local temple, spending the day in quiet meditation, observing a regime of simplicity and self-denial.

It sounds as if there is very little to see, but nothing could be farther from the truth. Vesak takes on a dramatically different quality after nightfall. As the full moon rises huge and yellow in the east, it is joined by countless earthbound lights. Every home, public square and place of business is festooned with illuminations: strings of fairy lights, traditional paper lanterns, oil lamps. In Colombo and the other big towns, the *pandals* begin to flicker and wink. Thousands of people take to the street to "see Vesak" — watch the folk plays enacted on village greens and open-air roadside stages, inspect the hawkers' wares and, of course, admire the illuminations.

Previous double page: The interior of a Buddhist temple, Bentota.
*All dressed up (**left**) for re procession at the Nawam Perahera,*
*Colombo. Lion flags (**above**) at Nawam, Colombo,*
signify Sinhalese nationalism.

Of these, the *pandals* are the main attraction. Great wooden screens sixty or seventy feet high, their painted panels tell stories from the life of the Buddha or from the *Jatakas*, in the serial manner of a comic-strip. The panels are the work of professional sign painters and are often very finely executed.

The real spectacle, however, is not the panels themselves, but the countless coloured lights that rim every one and form shifting, rotating patterns of ilumination around them. Large pandals may use upwards of fifty thousand lightbulbs, in every colour of the rainbow. The lighting sequence is controlled by an ingenious system of rotating drums etched with electrical contacts, a bit like oversized versions of antique phonograph cylinders. It is a complicated business and, in fact, it is usually the master electrician, not the carpenter or the sign painter, who is responsible for the pandal's ultimate design.

The most elaborate pandals, which symbolise hope, rise in the poorest areas of Colombo. The money to pay for them (often several hundred thousand rupees) is found by community subscription. It takes all year to collect enough. Every stallholder in the bazaar, every carpenter and cycle repairman, puts aside a rupee or two from each day's earnings. For these people, who feel the value of money acutely because they have almost none, the glittering pandal represents the sum of thousands of small, but real, sacrifices. Yet the money is given ungrudgingly, for the sake of the community. The pandal stands for a week or so, and is then pulled down.

The guidebooks tell visitors that Vesak is best spent in Colombo, where the illuminations may be seen in all their glory. If it is spectacle one is after, this is certainly true, for in the provinces, Vesak is a quiet time. Away from the brightness and clamour of the city, though, it is easier to appreciate the gentle, timeless nature of the festival.

The illuminations are different here. Every tiny garden glows with the light of simple paper lanterns, each containing one flickering candle. Doorsteps and verandahs are lined with tiny coconut-oil lamps made of clay, the incomparable *pol-thel-pahan*; the row of minute, yellow flames creates an effect utterly out of proportion to the simplicity with which it is achieved. The local temple, too, will be alive with their glow-worm flames, the light of piety itself.

Colombo at Vesak. A pandal rises above Thotalanga market in a fountain of light. The finest pandals are often erected in economically depressed areas, symbols of hope in slumland.

199

In the towns, as in Colombo, *dansalas*, stalls where passers-by are served a free meal, spring up. The dansalas are community charities, like the pandals, and are financed in much the same way. At one time it was impossible to pass a dansala without being made to step in and eat something. Nowadays the hospitality is not so insistent, but it is still there for all to partake of if they choose.

In the month of April, the sun enters the constellation Mesha, known to westerners as Aries. It is the time of the spring equinox and of the Sinhala and Tamil New Year.

Although it is a secular rather than a religious festival, *Avurudu* is kept with a fair amount of solemnity. The customs of the New Year are many and they are designed to ensure that the year will turn out well for the keepers. The annual ritual begins on New Year's Eve with a house-cleaning and lamp-lighting. The old year does not necessarily end at midnight, nor does the new one begin then; the actual times are arrived at by a set of astrological calculations. Between the end of the old year and the start of the new is a period of time that is outside time: the *nonagatha*. This period is a highly inauspicious one, and all activity comes to a halt; even the hearth is doused. At the end of the still time, the New Year proper begins.

It is heralded by the sound of the *raban*, a large drum played by several women at once. But the first ceremonial act of *Avurudu* is the lighting of the hearth (there is an astrologically-determined auspicious moment for this, and for every act that follows). After a ritual bath, everyone dresses in the colour of the New Year and 'sets to work'. Usually this is only a token effort, mere touching of the tools of one's trade, performed to ensure that good fortune will attend the year's labours. Next comes *ganu-denu*, an exchange of money, and finally an anointing ceremony. This is the moment of family reunion, when all transgressions are forgiven and the young offer betel-leaves to their elders as a mark of their respect. Afterwards, it is time to go visiting or step down to the village green where the traditional festive games will be in progress.

To an observer, one of the most remarkable things about Avurudu is the way it demonstrates the astrological bias of the Sri Lankan people. It has nothing to do with religion, for neither Buddhism, Hinduism, Islam nor Christianity specially encourage it; on the other hand, the old, earthy animism that is never far below the skin of even the most civilised of us must have something to do with it; certainly, Sri Lankan folk belief does attribute divine powers to the planets. But whatever the reason, astrology sits deep in the grain of Sri Lankan culture. Orthodox Sinhalese or Tamil parents would never dream of arranging marriages for their children without carefully examining the horoscope of the intended partner and comparing it with their own offspring's; any important venture, from buying a house to floating a company,

has a *nekatha*, a time the astrologer has deemed auspicious for its commencement. Once, the launch of a much-touted consumer product was delayed for over two months until the *nekatha* for the sales conference rolled around. The delay proved fatal: a competitor entered the market, and the product failed dismally.

The stars rule Sri Lanka closely and rigidly, through their representatives, the astrologers. The regency is a shared one, however, for palmistry, 'light-reading' and other methods of divination also prosper. It is an uncomfortable country for rationalists.

Roman Catholicism is the only Western faith to gain much of a purchase in Asia. Some ascribe this to the influence of the Portuguese who carried it eastward and did everything in their power to ensure that it took root and grew. For some reason, the Iberians seemed more prone to assimilation by their subject cultures than the North European colonialists who followed; both the Spanish in America and the Portuguese in Asia eventually "went native" so thoroughly that they became indistinguishable from the general population. Their religion, too, underwent the same process. Or did so, at least, as far as forms and observances go; the core of dogma remained unchanged (at least in our part of the world).

Whatever the reason, the vernacularisation of the church led to widespread adoption of local ritual. In Sri Lanka, this generally meant the absorption of Hindu and earlier, animistic ritual elements.

The result is a rich blend of faith and spectacle. In Sri Lanka, most Catholic shrines are on the west and northwest coasts of the island, reflecting the pattern of Portuguese settlement. The most important of them all is Madhu, near Mannar, where a great festival used to be held in former years. Lasting two weeks and involving thousands of pilgrims from all over the island, it showed the intimate connection of Catholicism with the Sri Lankan people in all its aspects. Sadly, the Madhu feast is no more; the fighting in the north has caused it to be abandoned.

But if Madhu, at least for the moment, is lost, there are for Sri Lanka's Catholics many other shrines. The faith remains strong, and that strength is demonstrated at the Feast of St. Anthony, at Kocchikade.

Kocchikade lies on the Colombo waterfront, in a maze of crowded, twisting streets lined with godowns and old row houses, once respectable but now terribly filthy and dilapidated. It is slumland, full of unlicensed taverns, bawdy-houses, gambling dens and poker-faced front doors behind which more exotic vices are accommodated. The old municipal fish market around the corner wafts a highly appropriate scent over the entire district. The Church of St. Anthony stands on the waterfront, its dignified facade contrasting vividly with the squalor surrounding it. Inside the church rests a statue of the island's favourite saint.

In Sri Lanka, boundaries of faith and dogma seem to matter very little, and St. Anthony, who is a reputed

A Kandyan drummer raps out a pade *(**left**). Great wheels of fire (**above**) make a* perahera *into pure spectacle at Nawam, Colombo.*

201

miracle-worker, is petitioned, not only by Catholics, but by everybody. He is the poor people's friend, and the fisherfolk love him; but on any day of the week one may encounter a Buddhist housewife, a Hindu lawyer or even a Muslim gem merchant kneeling before the statue of the saint. Ranks of candles, each representing a petition, burn at his feet.

St. Anthony's Feast is usually held in June. The preparations begin a few days earlier with the "mast-raising", a ceremony that has its roots in ancient shamanistic ritual but which was adopted by the church during the time when there were more parishes than priests and the latter did tours to visit all their charges; the mast was raised during the few days the priest was in residence at each church. Nowadays the practice has grown corrupt, and masts proliferate all along the route of the procession.

This begins at about six o'clock on the feast day. With elaborate care, St. Anthony is taken from the niche where he stands the rest of the year and placed on a draped and decorated float. A canopy supported by four brass poles covers his head. St. Anthony requires some protection from his followers; the crowds are held at bay by a six-hundred foot rope that maintains a clear area around the float. It is carried by several men from the nearby naval base. Within this mobile enclosure walk the priest and the various acolytes, choristers and other celebrants, along with assorted dignitaries and pressmen.

The route of the procession is strewn with leaves. As the statue passes through the streets, it is pelted with flowers, often whole garlands, so that soon the top of the float is thick with them. More substantial tributes are also offered and faintly through the noise of the crowd, comes a constant *chink-chink*, which one identifies after a while as the sound of coins striking the brass canopy supports around the saint.

The procession stops here and there along the way, sometimes for ceremonial reasons, sometimes simply because the press of bodies in those narrow streets has become too solid to penetrate. It takes hours to cover the entire route, although the actual distance is not long. By the time the journey is done, thousands of people will have paid their respects, and often shouted petitions, to Saint Anthony. The celebrants will be exhausted, but St. Anthony is indefatigable, as indeed he has to be, to deal with so many requests for favours; and soon enough, every-body's favourite saint will be back on his pedestal, giving ear once more to the pleas of the sick, the anxious and the distressed.

Hinduism must be the most complex religion on earth. No other faith so openly acknowledges the primal womb of folklore and magic that birthed it, yet Hinduism is anything but primitive: its thinkers have produced some of humanity's most advanced metaphysical speculation, and its cosmo-logy is so devastatingly accurate that modern physi-cists are only now discovering principles that have lain embedded in the Hindu myths for centuries. It is a religion with immense intellectual appeal, but it would be a sad mistake to approach it rationalistically. If anyone were tempted to try however, a visit to the nearest *kovil* would soon put him right.

Ideally, the kovil would be in Jaffna, and the visit take place between June and September. For those four months are the festival season on the peninsula, and the beauty and power of Shaivite Hinduism are at their peak. Nearly every Jaffna kovil holds its annual festival then, and the larger ones attract tens of thousands of devotees. The most impressive of them all is the festival at the kovil, or temple, in Nallur.

The Nallur kovil is dedicated to Kandasamy, or Murugan, better known in Sri Lanka as Skanda. Skanda is one of the tutelary deities of the island, and his seat is actually in the south, at Kataragama. However, he is

worshipped at other temples, most notably at Nallur. The 'Nallur Season' is a 26-day period in July and August, ending with the new moon. The daily *pujas* grow more and more crowded, but it is at night that the festival looks its best. Herbert Keuneman, an erstwhile Anglican priest and author of a five-volume manuscript on Sri Lanka, described it well:

> *"The ritual (is) florid to the point of prodigality, with its unfamiliar strident music of hautboys, drums and bells, with its mystic incenses and odours of jasmine and sandalwood and turmeric, yet saved from extravagance by its extraordinary instatement of simple but prodigious faith... The women barefoot and ankletted, their chignons looped in jasmine garlands... The men, bare to the waist in waist-cloths of white and sheer white shawls..."*

The climax of the proceedings is the arrival of the temple chariot. The *ratam* procession is not an everyday occurrence, but only takes place on special occasions. The gigantic car, several storeys tall, contains effigies of Murugan and his attendants, and is lavishly lit and decorated. It is drawn through the packed streets by dozens of bronzed and sweating men, dressed as Keuneman describes them, pulling on ropes as thick as a man's thigh. The prototype of the *ratam* is, of course, the monstrous Car of Jaganath, under whose wheels countless Indians sacrificed

themselves, until the British put a stop to the cruel practice and 'juggernaut' came to mean nothing more romantic than an articulated lorry. The Nallur chariots are less sanguinary vehicles; here an offering of sweat, rather than blood, is sufficient.

When the new moon rises, the ceremonies at Nallur end; but the Season of Skanda is not over yet. Kataragama is an old shrine, older than Nallur; so old, in fact, that no record of its building exists. One widely-accepted story is that King Dutugemunu built it, which would place its establishment somewhere in the second century BC; but Kataragama is obviously much older than this. Sri Lanka is full of places like it, places whose sanctity seems to antedate civilisation.

The deity to whom the shrine of Kataragama is dedicated is a war-god, and a god of wisdom, eldest son of Siva. Skanda, or Kartikeya, is said to have rested atop the mountain at Kataragma after a battle in which he defeated the *asuras*, the demons of Hindu mythology. The legend says he returned to the spot later and took a native girl as his bride.

Kataragama is much easier to reach now, for the jungle has been cleared beside the Menik Ganga, and wild animals are no longer a hazard, although malaria is still prevalent. However, convenience, or the lack of it, is the very last thing on the devotees' minds. Kataragama is the home of penance and of fantastic acts of self-mortification performed in the fulfilment of

*The Udappuwa festival is held over ten days in August and culminates in a remarkable firewalking ceremony in which the entire village participates. Devotees bring offerings (**left** and **above**) to the god Ganapati (Ganesh), who blesses the beginnings of new endeavours.*

vows. The war-god's demands are often terrible. Among the sweets, plastic bangles and other knick-knacks for sale on the hawkers' trays are steel hooks, skewers and similar instruments. There is no need to wonder at the use to which these are put, because examples of it are all around: men and women whose arms, backs, lips or tongues are perforated with them, and who dance ecstatic, oblivious to the pain, or transported by it. Some are actually carried suspended on trestles, their entire weight borne by hundreds of tiny hooks in their flesh.

There is a procession. The *puja* precedes it, and is attended by 'fire-swallowers' who carry pots of burning camphor. Once again, the "hautboys, drums and bells" sound again, along with the outcry from the pilgrims. But when the chief priest appears from within, silence falls. There is a lamp-lighting ceremony and an invocation. The priest then retires once more, to emerge again carrying the *yantra*, or relic of the god, in a closed casket. Neither the priest nor the casket is visible, for both are covered by a large sheet. Still shrouded, the priest mounts an elephant and is there-upon unveiled. The procession begins, the elephants, attendants and frantic devotees marching to wild music through the moonlit forest.

The *yantra* is carried to the Valliamma temple and it reposes there for a while; Kartikeya must be given some time to consort with his beloved mistress. Afterwards, the procession returns to the Kataragama Maha Devale, and the casket is replaced in the inner chamber, where none but the priest may enter.

On the final night of the festival, the fire-walking ceremony takes place. Everybody has heard about this, and everyone has a theory about how it is done. One thing is certain: the act is genuine. Those who "tread the flowers" are neither showmen nor professional ascetics; they are merely ordinary people facing an extraordinary test of faith. They have meditated for hours beforehand, bathed in the Menik Ganga and presented themselves, dripping, at the temple. When they invoke Agni and walk the fire, their faith is always rewarded. They neither feel the heat nor suffer so much as a blister.

Watching a miracle take place is a very curious experience. The 'fire' is a deep, long bed of glowing coals whose heat can be felt several yards away. The figures that walk or run across it are doing something one cannot possibly imagine onself being able to accomplish. There is no empathy with the firewalker, for the waking brain cannot understand what is happening; it takes a special state of mind to do that. To watch the firewalkers is to be reminded that the intellect is a very small pot and the phenomenal world an ocean it cannot possibly contain.

The festival ends the morning after, with a 'water-cutting' ceremony in the Menik Ganga. This is a significant and holy part of the Kataragama rites, and police keep the crowd from pressing too near. Afterwards, the pilgrims go home, and the ancient shrine in the jungle, so holy that no alteration can be made to its structure unless the god dictates it, grows silent and still. It will remain so until next August, when the Esala moon rises once more.

Every year, a cricket match is held between teams from two of Colombo's most exclusive boys' schools. It takes place amid scenes of festivity so abandoned that the game itself sometimes appears reduced to the status of a sideshow by comparison. It might seem odd that a mere school cricket match should provoke such frenzy, but Royal College and St. Thomas' College are not ordinary schools. Both were founded during the British occupation along the lines of the famous public schools of that country, and between them, they have educated a disproportionate share of Sri Lanka's most prominent citizens. Through these distinguished sons, the two colleges have touched every corner of the country's life. The Royal-Thomian, therefore, is something of a national event.

The first 'Battle of the Blues' was fought in 1880, and there has been one every year since. For three days in early March, all administrative, business and professional activity in Colombo is inconvenienced by the departure of key 'old boys' from their posts. Those not able to make it to the grounds remain distracted, one ear cocked to hear the voice of the radio commentator who is delivering a ball-by-ball description of the action on the field. Old jeeps and trucks festooned with giant flags (blue-and-black for St. Thomas', blue-and-gold for Royal) careen about the city streets, jammed with costumed schoolboys and raucous brass-and-drum bands. Acts of mad daredevilry become common, such as climbing a two-hundred-foot radio mast to tie one's school colours to the top. The municipal authorities cope with the situation with

as much good humour as they can muster and wait patiently for Sunday, when the madness will end.

Over the years, the Royal-Thomian has become encrusted with tradition. On the afternoon of the day preceding the great match, an impressive "cycle parade" takes place throughout the streets of the city. Once this was just what it says, a procession of flag-carrying schoolboys on push-bikes; now it is really a parade of trucks. Each school has its own parade, officially frowned upon but impossible to discourage, and these are carefully kept apart lest any ungentlemanly violence break out.

The next day, the grounds themselves become the focal point of all attention. The schoolboy spectators have a rough time of it, for they are mostly imprisoned behind steel mesh in what are laughingly called the "Boys' Tents". The rest of the stadium is thronged with singing, dancing, cheering representatives of all the ages of man, some with wives, sisters and girlfriends in tow. The more eminent old boys occupy the Colts' and Mustangs' tents. The Colts tend to be young, self-important and mercantile, the Mustangs older and mellowed. At the start of the first day's play everything looks orderly enough, but by afternoon, the mounting excitement, liberally fuelled with lashings of officially prohibited but openly-consumed drink, have reduced it to happy, riotous confusion. At lunch- and tea-time, when the players leave the field, the spectators occupy it themselves,

turning the cool green arena, temporarily bereft of its sauntering white-clad occupants, into a maelstrom of most un-British sweat, dust and garish colour.

By contrast, the match itself is often something of an anti-climax. School cricket is not the most absorbing game to watch, and Big Match nerves tend to make for safe rather than spectacular play. However, there are occasional moments of excitement, such as the match-saving last-wicket stand by St. Thomas' at the Centenary Encounter. By and large, while Royal and St. Thomas' have each won 30 matches (the figure is disputed), the awful consequences of losing usually cause games to be played to a draw, and there have been 48 of these.

But whatever the state of play on the field, the celebrations go on. The Royal-Thomian is a secular rite that arouses feelings of something that approaches religous fervour. Sri Lanka is now a Test Cricket country, but even the jet-setting glamour of international competition has not displaced the Royal-Thomian from its position as the nation's premier social event. And this is only fair, because there is probably nothing quite like it in all the world.

Dantapura was the capital of the ancient Indian kingom of Kalinga. The city took its name from the precious relic of the Buddha which was enshrined there: Dantapura means "City of the Tooth".

In the fourth century AD, Dantapura was besieged. The relic had to be saved, and so it was, hidden in a

Placing the Pol-thel-pahan, *coconut oil lamps that are "the light of piety", Kelaniya temple. The "paddy-heap" design of the stupa is clearly visible.*

princess' hair and smuggled out of the city. The princess arrived in Lanka and presented herself and her holy burden at the court of King Sri Meghavanna in Anuradhapura. It was in 313. Meghavanna was delighted and he housed the relic deep in the vaults of the Dhammachakra. To ensure that it received the veneration due to so holy an object, he then decreed that it be exhibited in procession once a year, heralded by elephants. The annual exhibition continued until Anuradhapura fell, more than six centuries later.

Today's Kandy Perahera continues the tradition instituted by Meghavanna, but is not a direct descendant of that ancient ritual. The Sacred Tooth disappeared from sight during the Polonnaruwa period and was only rediscovered some centuries later. Instead, the Esala Maha Perahera began as a Hindu festival, a procession in honour of the four tutelary deities of Kandy — Natha, Visnu, Skanda and Pattini. The Sacred Tooth is in fact a relative newcomer to the pageant.

It happened like this. By the late 18th century, the Buddhist *sangha* had fallen into decay, and no monk in the country was qualified to perform the rites of ordination. King Kirthi Sri Rajasinha solved the problem by importing a chapter of monks from Siam. The new arrivals were surprised at the pre-eminence of a Hindu festival in the capital of a Buddhist country. The king took their point and revived the Anuradhapura tradition; the sacred tooth, heralded by torch-wielding dancers and elephants, joined the Devale procession.

The same newborn August moon that heralds the end of the Nallur festival also signals the start of the Esala Perahera. The opening ceremonies involve the felling of a young *jak* or *esala* tree, which is split into four stakes. One of these is planted in the compound of each of Kandy's four 'tutelary' *devales*. The planting of the stakes represents a vow by all concerned that the *perahera* will be held.

The first five days see processions around the *kap* stakes as they stand in the *devale* compound. On the sixth night, these "devale peraheras" leave their temples and wind out on to the streets of Kandy, where they are joined by a larger perahera from the Dalada Maligawa, or Temple of the Tooth. The five nights of the Randoli Perahera, the grand procession that climaxes the fortnight-long festival, are bright with the light of the waxing moon. The last night, Esala Full Moon, features the most spectacular procession of all.

The Sacred Tooth takes precedence over the devale peraheras, and so the Maligawa Perahera leads the way. Actually, only a replica of the Tooth is caried in the perahera. The genuine relic, whose fate is said to be linked to that of the country, is far too precious to leave the Dalada Maligawa, and it reposes there within a series of locked, jewelled caskets, themselves all secured in an iron-barred cage. It is the replica, carried in a gorgeous illuminated reliquary on the back of a great tusked elephant, that receives the fervent salutations of the crowd.

This is how the Perahera proceeds: first come the whip-crackers, who herald the procession's arrival as they did the kings of old; next the flag-bearers; then the Peramuna Rala, riding the first elephant and holding in his hands the register of the Maligawa lands and the services due from their tenants; then Kandyan dancers, who step to the beat of traditional drums, the true indigenous music of Sri Lanka.

The drummers are playing the *gaman hewisi*, the war-march of the Sinhalese. They are followed by the Gajanayake Nilame, Master of the King's Elephants, carrying the silver goad that is his staff of office; then more elephants, dancers, drummers and officials, including the Master of Ceremonies, the Kariya Karana Rala. Following him is the Maligawa Tusker with his precious burden shaded under a mobile awning, accompanied by other grand elephants on either side and treading on a white cloth that is continually unrolled before his mighty feet and taken up again at the rear. After him come still more dancers and drummers and finally the temporal chief of the Maligawa, the Diyawadana Nilame, with his lancers and parasol-bearers.

Only then do the *devale* peraheras follow, each with its own elephants, one of whom carries the insignia of the god, and its own dancers, drummers and parasol-bearers. The character of each is slightly different, reflecting that of the deity it honours: the Kataragama Devale perahera, for example, features Tamil music and dancers. At the very end of the Perahera come the *randoli*, the temple palanquins which were said to carry the gods' invisible consorts, and are now used as repositories for the gifts and contributions of the crowd.

The Perahera ends with a water-cutting ceremony similar to that at Kataragama. It occurs in the early morning after the full moon, when the procession goes down to Katugastota. The waters of the Mahaveli Ganga are ritually cut with the sword of Kataragama, and a vessel full of river water carried back to the Natha Devale, where it will be preserved until the following year. After the day perahera that follows, the festivities end with a dance performed over the elephants' and dancers' trappings to ward off the Evil Eye. By then the spectators will have returned home to their villages and the tourists to whatever land these beings inhabit by custom.

The glory under the August moon is ended. The Holy of Holies has received the honour that is its due.

There are other festivals to tell of, but no space to tell them in. There is the Vel procession in Colombo, the Poson celebrations at Mihintale, the mass exorcisms at the church in Kudagama and a hundred others, large and small, many confined to a certain village, a certain temple, shrine or sacred spot.

There are the many Muslim festivals, celebrated in privacy with the prescribed minimum of outward show. The Prophet's Birthday, and the fast of Ramadan, and the feasting that ends it, are the only ones commonly known to infidels.

And the list goes on. Most of the festivals, though by no means all, have a religious nature. These are never empty mummeries; they are taken very seriously indeed by all those concerned.

One hears much of the exotic and colourful rites of Asia, but all too often the colours are acrylic, the exoticism contrived, the heart of what was once real and alive cut out, and a cash-box put in its place. It has not happened yet in Sri Lanka but, as we have said, this is a poor country, and the money which could be gained is an awful temptation.

To overcome it, there is only faith. And faith is hard to destroy, here where the old gods live. They are not domesticated, those ancient deities, and are not to be trifled with. They will not suffer dishonour without exacting a terrible vengeance.

*Passion play (**above**) at Pitipana, Negombo, to the north of Colombo.*
Note Veronica with handkerchief and the graphic touches.
***Following double page:** Mourners at the funeral of a popular*
Sinhalese film star and politician carry a poster showing
him in one of his most popular roles.

SITES

The footprints of history

THEY HAVE BEEN CLIMBING ALL NIGHT, AND now it is drawing near dawn. Exhausted as they are, the pilgrims must hurry; otherwise the sun will be up in the sky before they reach the top of the mountain. Already, the black cone of the peak is gathering definition against the lightening sky. In the forest below, the birds have begun to sing. The summit is cold and swept by the harsh wind. It is also crowded, for many pilgrims have attained it during the course of

the night and there is little room for laggards. Somehow, like seabirds on a cliff, the newcomers find a purchase and settle themselves down.

They do not have long to wait. The eastern sky is glowing: suddenly, a fiery crack appears between earth and sky. On Adam's peak, the sun has risen. No one is watching.

Instead, all eyes are resolutely turned westward, where something far stranger is taking place. The Peak is casting its shadow upon the very air. The cone of darkness mounts up to heaven right in front of the pilgrims' eyes; it is a signal from the sacred mountain to the gods themselves. The watchers on the summit have their personal messages to add to that mystic communication; cries of holy joy rend the air.

Adam's Peak is the most sacred place in Sri Lanka and, indeed, it has some claim to being the holiest in the world. If a sanctity that transcends the boundaries of any one faith will substantiate the claim, we may consider it proved, for no less than four great religions, as well as a number of lesser sects, regard the mountain as a holy shrine. Buddhists call it Sri Pada. To them the object of veneration, an enormous 'footprint' impressed in the rock at the summit of the 2,300m peak, is the mark the Buddha left behind to commemorate his third visit to his beloved Lanka. To Hindus, the footprint is Siva's. Eastern Christians attribute it to St. Thomas the Apostle, for there is a legend that he visited here. But the most charming tale of the footprint is the one told by the Muslims, who say it is Adam's. After his expulsion from Paradise, the Father of Men stood penance atop the peak for a thousand years, poised on one foot all the time. Afterwards, we are relieved to hear, he was reunited with Eve atop Mt. Arafat, near Mecca.

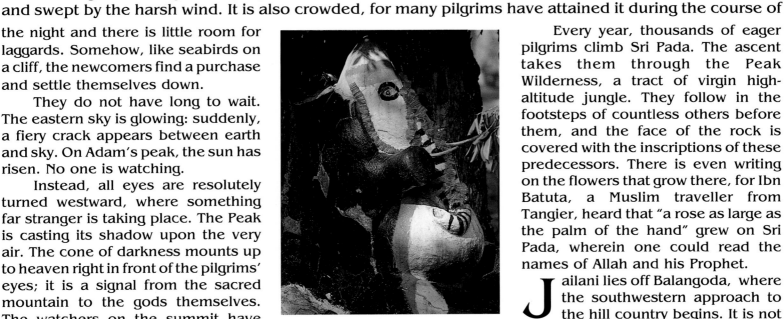

Every year, thousands of eager pilgrims climb Sri Pada. The ascent takes them through the Peak Wilderness, a tract of virgin high-altitude jungle. They follow in the footsteps of countless others before them, and the face of the rock is covered with the inscriptions of these predecessors. There is even writing on the flowers that grow there, for Ibn Batuta, a Muslim traveller from Tangier, heard that "a rose as large as the palm of the hand" grew on Sri Pada, wherein one could read the names of Allah and his Prophet.

Jailani lies off Balangoda, where the southwestern approach to the hill country begins. It is not hard to reach the shrine; a good road takes the pilgrim most of the way there, and even the last mile or two of jungle footpath is fairly easy to go along. However, despite its accessibility, it is not a very well-known spot, except to devout Muslims, who go there on pilgrimage for they look upon it as a holy place.

There are no splendid monumental ruins or ancient artworks at Jailani. Nor do miracles happen there every day. It is simply a place where a Mohammedan saint lived and meditated. All the same, there is no mistaking Jailani's significance. Its physical location leaves the visitor no room for doubt.

The shrine, with its rudimentary shelter for pilgrims and a few small shops that open during the season, nestles in a small triangular valley. But we need only climb the modest-looking hill opposite before sunrise, and dawn will reveal a spectacular vision. For the other side of the hill is a precipice several hundred feet high. Jailani is an eyrie, a spur outthrust from the great central massif of the island, and the view from the top of the hill is simply magnificent. On the left, and slightly behind, tower

*Previous double page: Buddhist monks walk past a Hindu kovil in Trincomalee. Novice monks (**left**) at Ras Vehera, near Aukana. Sri Lankan religious feeling is very much tied up with the beauties of the diverse landscape. The roadside Ganapati image (**above**) powerfully recalls Hinduism's animistic roots.*

those enormous cloud-clothed ramparts. Ahead are the southern plains and an uninterrupted view for fifty miles, all the way to the distant ocean. The sight makes a mockery of the everyday world and its concerns; this, one feels, is how God must see his creation.

The place still draws hermits to it, and there were five in residence at the shrine only a couple of years ago. One had taken a fourteen-year vow of silence, but he could communicate quite well by making use of signs and by using his expressive eyes. Another one shared his cave with a cobra.

There are places on earth where the skin of everyday events grows so transparent that one may catch a glimpse of the mystery underneath. It is not just a matter of folklore, for every spot on earth where man has dwelt is thick with legend; nor is it a question of sanctity, although such places do tend to be seen as being sacred and are revered as such. Perhaps it has something to do with the environment, some mystic geometry that triggers a response in parts of the mind we have lost, or are only beginning to gain, the use of. All attempts at explaining the mystery lapse into mumbo-jumbo sooner or later, so it is better not to try. Still, there is no denying that the phenomenon exists.

Islands seem to have some special power to evoke the response: look at Easter Island, Bali, even Britain — at least, the parts of it not yet encased in concrete. Then look at Sri Lanka.

The island is enchanted. It has been called the "Kingdom of Demons" and the "Paradise of Adam". It draws sensitive visitors irresistibly to it like a magnet, and often they cannot go home again. It has been a battleground for heroes and a refuge for pilgrims. It is one of the few places left on earth where the gods, and their opposite, are still truly alive.

Like all magical places, the Resplendent Isle is seen at its best by moonlight. Naturally, every full moon day is a national holiday in Sri Lanka. As the silver light touches the ruined pillars of the Brazen Palace, or brushes the sleeping countenance of an old stone Buddha, or flings a shining bridge from the far horizon to a phosphorescent beach fringed with thick jungle, the wonder and mystery rise to the surface once more. In the moonlight, it is easy to see why, of all the beauties of the earth, the Isle of Lanka was the only one the Buddha, he who was free from all attachment, loved and protected.

"I am Al-Jailani, my name is Muhiyuddin, and my banners fly from the mountain-tops." Islam's principal saint and his followers rested at Kaltota (Jailani) after a pilgrimage to Adam's Peak, where Adam rested after being expelled from Paradise. **Following double page**: The Valley of Badulla is covered with mist at dawn.

THE JOURNEY'S END
Thoughts on the passage

THE VOYAGE UP THE RIVER IS ALMOST OVER. Where has it ended? It would be nice to pretend we've reached the source of the stream, but that, of course, is nonsense. No one has ever discovered it; we only know the general direction in which it lies, up there among the forests of history, myth and folklore, where only the most resourceful and determined explorers can penetrate. You can't take a canoe up there, let alone a riverboat. Let's say that we've

reached the practical limit of navigation, given the size and displacement of our vessel.

Do river-pilots get enthusiastic about their jobs? This one would certainly have liked to spend some more time on the journey, to linger a little over the wonders that line the bank, follow one or two intriguing tributaries just to see where they lead. But that would be self-indulgent, and possibly hard on the passengers.

Already one can feel a touch of apprehension among them for, as the boat edges closer to the landing-stage, it is clear that all is not well on shore. From up ahead, just beyond the bank and over the ridge, disturbing reports reach our ears; was that the sound of gunfire? Is there a war being waged on land?

Change, having passed Sri Lanka by for so long, is now making up for lost time. The forces that kept the nation and her people sheltered from the full impact of global culture are really too numerous and complex to explain here, but there are some hints that can be found to explain the kind of cultural isolation that helps explain what Sri Lanka is facing today.

Some of the factors were political, some economic. The state of mass communications probably had a lot to do with it — there is only one state-run radio station in the whole country; no television till 1978. A disastrous experiment with the lunar calendar which had us working while the rest of the world took its weekend and vice versa, probably helped also. The strong grip of traditional culture on the attitudes of the people was a more positive factor that nevertheless contributed to the same result.

Everywhere you look, traditional patterns are being replaced by new ones. It is a sort of revolution, and like all revolutions, it is traumatic. Coping with the

trauma has become Sri Lanka's first great test as an independent, modern nation. From a historical perspective, it is not hard to be optimistic. In two and a half thousand years, we have been through a lot, and we're still here — all of us together. We have weathered natural disasters, internal divisions, foreign invasions, epidemics, even "the most dangerous moment" of the Second World War. Provided the decision isn't taken out of our hands by the Nuclear Club, we'll probably survive the Twentieth Century without too much trouble. It'll change us, of course, all those other experiences did, too. They made us what we are.

But while the historical perspective is fine for historians, it provides cold comfort for those actually in the throes of transition. People who knew only one way to live are now confronted by evidence of many others. They suspect that some of them might be possible alternatives to their own lifestyles. The only way to be sure, however, is to try the experiment and find out for themselves. Women, specially, have to face different choices. They are now aware that they need not endure the traditional fate of their mothers.

"Shall I wear a dress instead of a sari? It looks pretty, but will mother think me immodest?" "Shall I take a job in a garment-factory or try for a diploma of accountancy?"

"In the old days I'd have had to stay home and get married at nineteen, but now I can afford to wait a bit longer. Maybe I'll even look for a husband myself, instead of leaving it to my parents... but will they approve? What will I do if they don't?"

A new consciousness is sweeping the land. People are starting to ask questions about themselves, their lives and their place in the world.

*Previous double page: The chaitiya of a village temple at Vesak. Inner Chamber (**left**) at the Houses of Parliament, Kotte. The building is the work of modern Sri Lanka's most famous architect, Geoffrey Bawa. The silver palmleaf chandelier is by Laki Senanayake. Camphor flares (**above**) on a coconut at a Hindu kovil.*

The answers are not always what they should be; like all emerging societies, Sri Lanka has her fair share of injustices and inequalities. It takes time to resolve them peacefully; some people do not have the patience, and that is how the fighting begins. Violence rarely provides a satisfactory solution to anything; it is far more likely to make the problem worse; but try telling that to an angry man.

Until the echoes of the cultural collision die away and the rate of social change stabilises, Sri Lanka is going to be an exhilarating but uncomfortable country to live in. It will remain a beautiful country to visit, and a safe one too, provided the visitor is not reckless. We don't care to involve our guests in family quarrels.

The journey upriver has been a voyage of discovery for the author as much as for the reader. Few people are called upon to make a survey of their country and people in this fashion: I recommend the exercise to anyone suffering the pangs of dislocation (a common late-twentieth-century ailment).

There were times when I felt as if I were discovering Sri Lanka for the first time. There were others when I wondered if I were doing so just in time to lose her forever. So, as the riverboat ties up and the passengers start to disembark, the native pilot has learned something too, and would like to end his voyage with a word to his fellow-natives.

We live, as the old Chinese curse has it, in interesting times. It sounds pompous, but this may be one of the turning-points of our nation's history. If that is the case, then it behooves us to conduct ourselves thoughtfully, because for better or worse the future is being shaped by our actions today.

The things of the past often seem outmoded and irrelevant, but there is wisdom in the old ways. I am not suggesting we return to them wholesale; that would be foolish sentimentality, perhaps a kind of madness, a futile attempt to turn back the clock. The trick, I believe, is to extract the wisdom embedded in the old traditions and adapt it to our own ends.

It is natural that we should be impatient to lay our hands on the good things we have never had. It is right that we should burn to set twisted matters straight. It is no sin to catch the flood-tide as it rises. But in our eagerness to get things shipshape, we had better be careful about what we throw over the side. There may well be sapphires among the jetsam.

Festival time at the Church of St. Anthony, Kocchikade. Note the
mobile altar and the mast. St. Anthony of Padua is the Sri Lankan
people's favourite saint. **Following double page**: Anuradhapura sunset. **At left,** the newly-restored Ruwanweliseya Dagoba recalls the
days of King Dutugemunu; **at right**, the ruined Jetavana Chaitiya.

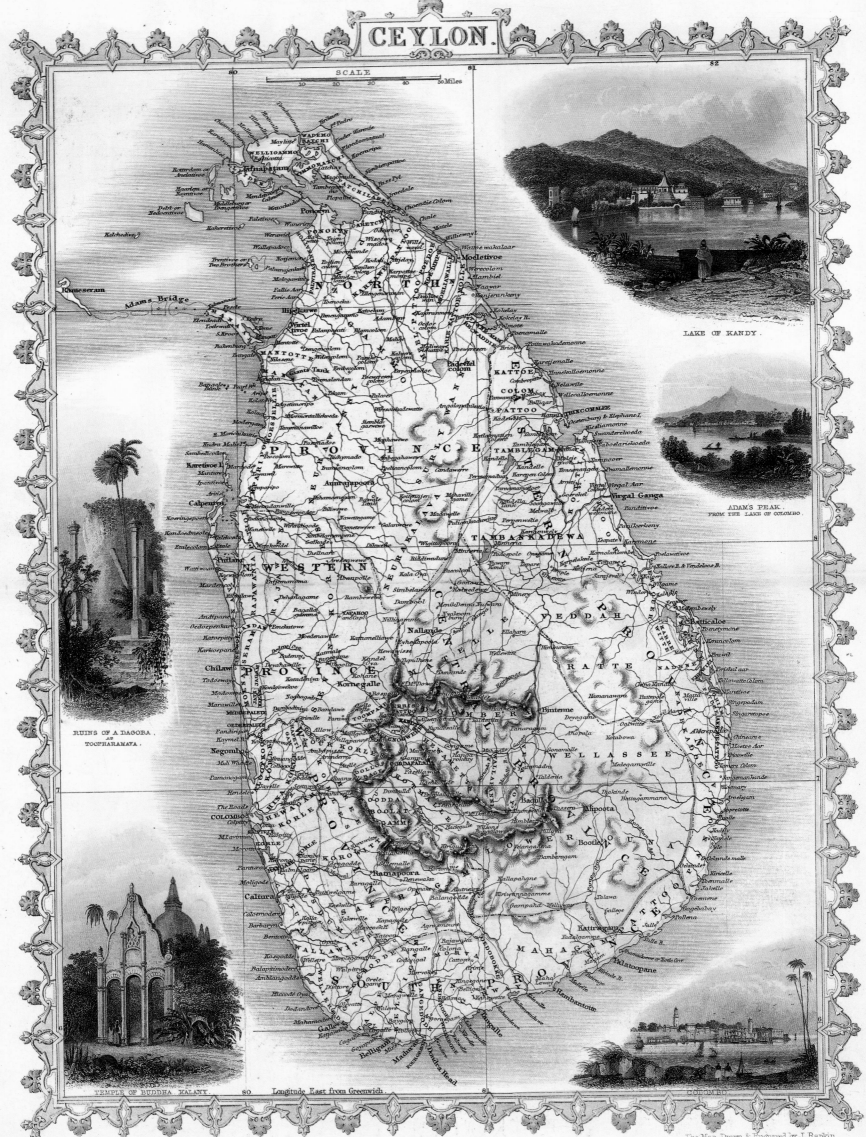

CEYLON.

SCALE
10 20 30 40 50 Miles

LAKE OF KANDY.

ADAM'S PEAK,
FROM THE LAKE OF COLOMBO.

RUINS OF A DAGOBA
AT TOOPHARAMAVA.

TEMPLE OF BUDDHA KALANY.

COLOMBO.

Longitude East from Greenwich.

The Illustrations Drawn & Engraved by H. Winkles.

The Map Drawn & Engraved by J. Rapkin.

APPENDICES

HISTORICAL CHRONOLOGY

BIBLIOGRAPHY AND FILMOGRAPHY

GLOSSARY

INDEX

ACKNOWLEDGMENTS

__Left__: Map drawn and engraved by J Rapkin, from "The Illustrated Atlas and Modern History of the World" edited by R Montgomery Martin and published by John Tallis in 1851.

500,000 BC Estimated. first arrival of humans on the island of Ceylon.

6th & 5th centuries BC Arrival in Lanka of the first N. Indian colonists, who later become the Sinhalese people.

483 BC (est.) Buddha passes away. This event is said to be contemporaneous with Vijaya's arrival in Lanka.

c. **350 BC** Sinhalese capital is moved from Upatissagama to Anuradhapura under King Pandukabhaya.

268 BC After a bloody fraternal struggle, Prince Asoka attains imperial Maurya throne in India. Later he renounces violence and becomes an ardent Buddhist. Sends his son (or brother) Mahinda to preach Buddhism in Lanka.

250–210 BC Reign of Devanampiya Tissa in Lanka. Mahinda's mission arrives at Mihintale. King Tissa is the first convert; he builds Thuparama, first of the great stupas, to enshrine collarbone-relic of the Buddha.

205–161 BC Reign of Elara, Tamil ruler of great fame. Ruled justly and fairly for 44 years until re-establishment of Sinhalese rule by Dutugemunu.

161–137 BC Reign of Dutugemunu. He builds Mirisvetiya, Lohapasada monastery, Ruwanweliseya.

c. **80 BC** Vattagamini Abhaya (Valagamba) builds Abhayagiri *vihare* on site of earlier Jain monastery in fulfilment of a vow. New monastery becomes centre of schismatic Buddhist sect, often called Mahayanist, as opposed to Mahavihare doctrines. The conflict will continue, often bloodily, until Parakramabahu the Great unifies the Sangha in 1165.

AD 112 Accession of Gajabahu I. He attended dedication of Pattini *kovil* in the S. Indian capital and later establishes temple to her in Lanka.

276–303 Reign of Mahasena, the great irrigationist who built Minneriya tank and the last of the Mahavamsa kings. Rivalry, between Mahavihare and Abhayagiri sects result in near civil war during his reign. Now deified and worshipped at Minneriya.

303–331 Reign of Sri Meghavanna. Arrival of the Sacred Tooth at Anuradhapura.

411 Arrival of Fa Hsien, Chinese Buddhist monk who lived in Lanka two years and described life there in his writings.

459–477 Reign of Dhatusena, founder of the Moriya dynasty. Built one tank for each year of his reign, including the famous Kalawewa. Murdered by his son, Kassapa.

477–495 Reign of Kassapa I. Builder of Sigiriya, one of the real wonders of the ancient world. Killed by his half-brother, Moggalana.

495–512 Reign of Moggalana I. Inditing of the *Mahavamsa* begins, drawing and expanding on earlier literary sources. Cruelty to Kassapa's followers earned him the nickname *rakshasa* (demon).

9th century Probable period of establishment of Kalingan dynasty in Jaffna by Uggirasingham.

993 Chola invasion under King Rajaraja I sacks and burns Anuradhapura. Rajarata (North & Central Lanka) becomes a Chola province, administered from the new capital, Polonnaruwa.

1017 Chola expedition to Ruhuna (S. Lanka) captures Sinhalese king Mahinda V. He dies at Polonnaruwa in 1029, and unrest over Chola occupation begins.

1055–1110 Reign of Vijayabahu I, possibly the greatest Sinhalese warrior-king. Assumes Ruhuna throne aged 18 after childhood spent in jungle refuges learning guerrilla tactics at first hand. Challenges Chola empire and, despite treachery within own greatly inferior forces, captures Polonnaruwa in 1067, only to lose it again almost at once. Succeeds in liberating both Polonnaruwa and Anuradhapura in 1070. Crowned again in Anuradhapura, moves court to Polonnaruwa in 1074. Restores debilitated *Sangha* through mission to Burma.

1153–1186 Reign of Parakramabahu the Great. Begins preparations for unifying country while still in teens. Comes to throne of Dhakkinadessa (SW Lanka) about 1140. After making it the most powerful principality, moves against Rajarata. Captures Polonnaruwa, treating former ruler Gajabahu with kindness, then repulses attack by Ruhuna kings to make himself king of all Lanka. Reign notable for great public works, social, cultural and military achievements. Mends old rifts in the *Sangha* with the Unification of 1165.

13th century Tamil-speaking peoples occupy all of Jaffna and the Vanni. Collapse of Pandya sea power sees region become an independent kingdom under its Arya Chakravarti rulers.

1215–1256 Reign of Magha, or Kalinga Vijayabahu, who invades Lanka with 24,000 troops. There is some uncertainty as to invader's origin: according to some sources, 'Kalinga' was actually the Sumatran kingdom of Srivijaya; others say it was a region of that name in S. India. Traditionally, Magha is said to have instituted a reign of terror, letting his soldiers have their way with the local population, plundering monasteries and turning them into barracks, burning books and performing acts of rape and torture. However, some Sinhalese chronicles disagree and ascribe these occurrences to the years before the arrival of Magha.

1232–1236 Reign of Vijayabahu III. He moves the Sinhalese capital to Dambadeniya. Rajarata still under Magha.

1284 Mission from Kublai Khan in China seeks to carry home Tooth and Bowl relics of the Buddha, but returns empty-handed.

c. **1293** Arrival of Marco Polo, who spends some time as guest of king of Jaffna, but does not travel in Lanka.

1344 Accession of Parakramabahu IV. The court is moved to Gampola, in the hill country.

1371–1408 Reign of Buvanaikabahu V. Capital moved again, this time to Sri Jayawardanapura, or Kotte, a site surrounded by marshes and therefore easily defensible.

1412–1467 Reign of Parakramabahu VI. He rebuilds Kotte and houses the Tooth Relic there. War on Jaffna ends victoriously around 1450. Sapumal Kumaraya, leader of the Sinhalese forces, is installed as regent of Jaffna. At the end of Parakramabahu's reign, he returns to Kotte to be crowned King Buvanaikabahu VI.

1505 Portuguese fleet under Dom Lourenço de Almeida drops anchor in Colombo. Later, a Portuguese fort is built there.

1521 Partition of Kotte kingdom into three rival principalities leads to emergence of kingdom of Sitawak, which soon makes inroads into Kotte territory. In following years, alliances and enmities amongst Kotte, Sitawaka and Udarata will shift constantly, with the Portuguese backing one or another as convenient to their own interests.

1544 Massacre of Catholic converts on the island of Mannar by king of Jaffna.

1553 Vidiye Bandara, a Kotte nobleman, escapes from gaol. Exploits reaction against Catholicism to launch revolt against the Portuguese. Rebellion quashed in 1555 by Sitawaka–Portugal alliance. Vidiye Bandara seeks refuge in Jaffna, where he dies in a quarrel.

1580 King Dharmapala of Kotte passes his kingdom to the Portuguese Crown.

1591 Portuguese force under Andre Furtado de Mendoza kills king of Jaffna and replaces him with a puppet.

1594 Fall of Sitawaka. Kotte restored as Portuguese subject state. Centre of Sinhalese resistance moves to Kandy.

27 May 1597 On death of Dharmapala, Kotte proclaimed a possession of the Portuguese Crown by Captain–General Jeronimo de Azavedo.

1621 Annexation of Jaffna to Portugal by Captain–General Constantine de Sa.

1633 Portuguese–Kandyan treaty grants East Coast ports to Portugal.

1638 Rajasinha II of Kandy signs treaty with VOC: monopoly of spice trade and all expenses paid in exchange for aid in ousting the Portuguese.

June 1658 Jaffna surrenders, ending Portuguese presence in Ceylon. East Coast ports returned to Kandy. VOC presents a bill of 7,265,460 guilders to Rajasinha II for finishing the job.

1739 Death of Narendrasinha, last Sinhalese king of Kandy. His successor and relative by marriage, Vijaya Rajasinha, is first of Nayakkar dynasty.

1750 Kirthi Sri Rajasinha sends mission to Thailand. Mission returns in 1753 and ordinations begin.

1795 The 'Kew Letter' by the Dutch refugee Stadholder cedes all Dutch colonial possession to Britain.

12 Oct 1798 Former Dutch possessions in Ceylon become British territories jointly administered by the Crown and the British East India Company.

Dec 1796 Rebellion breaks out over certain British tax and social reforms. Ends in 1798 after new measures are revoked.

1 Jan 1802 British territories become the Crown Colony of Ceylon, with Sir Frederick North the Governor.

1803–1805 First Kandyan War.

19 Jan 1815 News of the capture of Sri Wickrama Rajasinha, the last King of Kandy, is brought to Governor Robert Brownrigg. Intrigues between the British and Sinhalese feudal chiefs have put an end to the kingdom of Kandy.

1817–1818 The Great Rebellion against the British is led by dispossessed Kandyan chieftains and is quashed.

1823 First coffee plantation set up at Sinhapitiya by George Bird.

1831–1832 Colebrooke–Cameron Commission recommends a liberal, *laissez-faire* system of government and administration, with *rajakariya* abolished.

1869 First appearance of the coffee-rust fungus, which will wipe out the coffee plantations and several fortunes.

11 Dec 1919 First session of newly-formed Ceylon National Congress under Sir Ponnambalam Arunachalam. Congress wants larger role for Ceylonese in country's government.

July 1928 A commission headed by the Earl of Donoughmore examines the 1924 Constitution and declares it "an unqualified failure". Proposes measures aimed at ultimate self-determination for the Ceylonese. Its crucial recommendation is the introduction of universal suffrage; 'universal', that is, except for Tamil labour and adult women under 25.

20 Mar 1931 Old Legislative Council dissolved; in its place is a largely elected State Council, with ministers heading committees responsible for the administration of Home Affairs, Agriculture and Lands, Local Administration, Labour, Industry and Commerce, Education, Communication and Works.

18 Dec 1935 Formation of the Lanka Sama Samaja Party, the first Ceylonese Marxist party. Two members became State Councillors in 1936 Elections.

April 1942 Attacks on Colombo (5 April) and Trincomalee (9 April) by Japanese aircraft. British shipping suffers most.

Feb 1944 D S Senanayake presents a draft Constitution to his fellow Ministers in the State Council.

22 Dec 1944 The Soulbury Commission arrives in Ceylon to "examine and discuss any proposals for constitutional reform in the Island".

31 Oct 1945 The British government, in a White Paper, offers Ceylon a Constitution based on Lord Soulbury's 'recommendations'.

24 Sept 1947 D S Senanayake elected Prime Minister under the Soulbury Constitution.

4 April 1948 Birth of the Independent Dominion of Ceylon. Sir Henry Moore, former Governor, sworn in as Governor–General. D S Senanayake heads first independent government.

12 Aug 1953 Islandwide *hartal*, or strike, in response to reduction in rice subsidy results in declaration of state of Emergency and widespread violence; many police shootings.

April 1956 Year of the Buddha Jayanthi, or 2500th anniversary of Buddhism, sees upsurgence of ethnic-religious tension and a General Election in which UNP suffers its first defeat. A coalition government, the Mahajana Eksath Peramuna (MEP), headed by S W R D Bandaranaike, takes power.

25 Sep 1959 Prime Minister S W R D Bandaranaike assassinated by a *bikkhu*. Emergency declared again, MEP government resigns.

Oct 1964 Pact between Prime Ministers Sirima Bandaranaike of Ceylon and Lal Bahadur Shastri of India arranges for repatriation of 525,000 Indian Tamil estate workers over 15 years; 300,000 will become Ceylon citizens.

Apr 1971 Armed insurrection by Janatha Vimukthi Peramuna (JVP) fails for lack of popular support. JVP leader Rohana Wijeweera and others gaoled.

22 May 1972 Dominion of Ceylon becomes Democratic Socialist Republic of Sri Lanka. Former Governor–General Sir William Gopallawa becomes the first President.

4 Apr 1978 Under a constitutional amendment, J R Jayawardene becomes the first Executive President of Sri Lanka.

General Works

An Account of the Interior of Ceylon and of its Inhabitants, with travels in that island by John Davy, MD, FRS. London, 1821. An early description of Ceylon, its geography, natural history and people; excellent close observation. John Davy, brother of Sir Humphrey, served in Ceylon as army surgeon and physician-in-attendance to Governor Brownrigg between 1817 and 1819.

Ceylon: An Account of the Island *etc.* by Sir James Emerson Tennent. Tisara Publications, Colombo, 1971 (orig. pub. London, 1857). Arguably the most comprehensive of the early accounts of Sri Lanka. Tennent, a Colonial Secretary in Ceylon, writes clearly and knowledgeably.

A Handbook for the Ceylon Traveller. A Studio Times publication, Colombo, 1974. The Sri Lankan traveller's companion. Knowledgeable, comprehensive and opinionated. Every imaginable aspect of country and culture is treated; a treasure trove of fascinating detail.

Insight Guide: Sri Lanka. Based on a manuscript by Herbert Keuneman. Apa Productions, Hong Kong, 1983. Colourful, comprehensive guidebook. Keuneman's original manuscript was a labour of love, fruit of a lifetime's intimate study of the people and the country.

The View From Serendip by Arthur C Clarke. Random House, New York, 1977. Notes on life on Serendip and other matters by the famous science and science-fiction writer.

History

A Concise History of Ceylon from Earliest Times to the Arrival of the Portuguese in 1505 by C W Nicholas and Senarat Paranavitana. Ceylon University Press, Colombo, 1961.

An Historical Relation of the Island of Ceylon in the East-Indies by Robert Knox. Richard Chiswell, London, 1681 (repr. Tisara Publications, 1966). Knox, son of the master of the British merchant ship *Ann*, was a captive of the King of Kandy from 1659 to 1679. His account of that captivity is absorbing and historically priceless. An abridgement, ***Robert Knox in the Kandyan Kingdom***, edited by E F C Ludowyk with photographs by Lionel Wendt (Oxford University Press, London, 1948) is more accessible than the original.

Ancient Jaffna by Mudaliyar C Rasanayagam. Asian Educational Services, New Delhi, 1984. A good overview of the subject, although the final word on Jaffna's early history is very far from being written.

A Record of Buddhistic Kingdoms, trans. James Legge. Clarendon Press, Oxford, 1886 (repr. Dover Publications, New York, 1965). An account by the Chinese monk Fa-Hien (Fa Hsien) of his travels in India and Ceylon in the 4th and 5th centuries AD in search of the Buddhist Books of Discipline. Interesting descriptions of life in fifth-century Anuradhapura.

A Reign of Ten Kings by Nalini de Lanerolle. Ceylon Tourist Board, Colombo, 1985. An easy, informative comparative study of Sri Lanka and world history, useful for placing events on the island in a wider historical context.

Culavamsa, vols. 1 & 2, trans. Wilhelm Geiger. Ceylon Government Information Dept, Colombo, 1953.

Glimpses from the Past of the Moors of Ceylon ed. Marikar, Lafir and Macan Markar. Moors' Islamic Cultural Home, Colombo, 1977. A collection of newspaper articles on the community, its origins and history.

Mahavamsa, trans. Wilhelm Geiger. Ceylon Government Information Dept, Colombo, 1912.

The Historic Tragedy of the Island of Ceilao by Joao Ribeiro; trans. P E Pieris. 4th Edition, Lake House, Colombo, 1948. Generally considered to be the first European account of the island, by a Portuguese soldier who served there from 1640 to 1658.

The Modern History of Ceylon by E F C Ludowyk. 1966. The British period and after, up to the mid-1960s. Good source for political and constitutional history.

The Most Dangerous Moment by Michael Tomlinson. William Kimber, London, 1976. An account of the Japanese attacks on Colombo and Trincomalee, and of the events leading up to them.

The Story of Sigiri by Senarat Paranavitana. Lake House, Colombo, 1972. Based on and consisting largely of documents prepared by Anandasthavira, a historian and archaeologist active during the reign of Parakramabahu VI. A well-reasoned and documented retelling of the Sigiriya story, which differs from the ***Mahavamsa*** version.

Natural History

A Guide to the Birds of Ceylon by G M Henry, illustrated by the author. A classic. Henry's ornithological portraits have inspired a generation of artists and nature-lovers.

Birds of Sri Lanka by T S U de Zylva. Trumpet Publishers, Colombo, 1984. Photographic portraits in colour, with an informative and knowledgeable text.

Jungle Tide by John Still. Blackwood & Sons, London, 1947. A collection of poetically written essays on Sri Lankan wildlife and culture, noteworthy for their factual accuracy and literary value. Several poems interpolated with text.

Agriculture

A Hundred Years of Ceylon Tea by D M Forrest. Chatto & Windus, London, 1967. A well-written

Zodiac sign on a temple ceiling.

insider's look at the Ceylon tea trade; absorbing material.

Sociology & Anthropology

Aspects of Sinhalese Culture by Martin Wickramasinghe. Colombo, Tisara Publishers, 1952. Cultural notes by the famous Sinhalese novelist.

Ceylon — A Pictorial Survey by M D Raghavan. M D Gunasena, Colombo, 1962. A popular treatment of the subject by a noted anthropologist and ethnologist.

Tamil Culture in Ceylon: A General Introduction by M D Raghavan. Kalai Nilayam, Colombo, 1971.

Cookery

Ceylon Cookery by Chandra Dissanayake. Author's copyright; Colombo, 1968. Comprehensive.

'The Ceylon Daily News' Cookery Book by Hilda Deutrom. The Associated Newspapers of Ceylon Limited, Colombo, 1929 (5th Edition, 1964). The indispensable Sri Lankan housewife's companion!

Arts & Crafts

Design Elements in Sri Lankan Temple Paintings by L T P Manjusri. Archaeological Society of Sri Lanka, Colombo, 1977. The only published examples of Manjusri's temple copyings. A wealth of material remains unpublished.

Mediaeval Sinhalese Art by Ananda K Coomaraswamy. 2nd Edition, Pantheon Books, New York, 1956. Still the standard text on Sri Lankan arts and crafts, its scope is considerably wider than the title suggests. The author was one of the leading figures of modern Sri Lankan culture.

The Arts and Crafts of India and Ceylon by Ananda K Coomaraswamy. Farrar Straus, New York, 1964 (orig. pub. 1913). An early

work, full of provocative ideas and insights.

The Vernacular Architecture of Sri Lanka by Barbara Sansoni, Laki Senanayake and Ronald Lewcock. Forthcoming.

Dance & Drama

Sinhala Natum: Dances of the Sinhalese by M D Raghavan. M D Gunasena, Colombo, 1967. A scholarly treatment of all major Sinhalese dance forms.

Sokari of Sri Lanka by M H Goonetilleka. Dept. of Cultural Affairs Publications, Colombo, 1976.

The Sinhalese Folk Play and the Modern Stage by Ediriweera Sarathchandra. Ceylon University Press, Colombo, 1953. Sarathchandra is the leading authority on Sri Lankan folk theatre.

Festivals

The Kandy Esala Perahera by Sir Richard Aluwihare, KCMG, CBE. M D Gunasena, Colombo, 1952. A comprehensive descriptive account of the *Perahera* and its origins.

Fiction

An Anthology of Sinhalese Literature up to 1815 selected by the UNESCO National Commission of Ceylon, ed. Christopher Reynolds. George Allen and Unwin, London, 1970. Suffers from uneven quality of translation; nevertheless, it is a good introduction to the literature, including extracts from such classics as *Guttiliya*, *Salalihini Sandesaya*, *Ummaggajatakaya* and the Sigiri graffitti.

Colombo Heat by Christopher Hudson. Macmillan, London, 1986. Novel set in 1942 Ceylon. A well-researched, vivid picture of life in the country before and during the Japanese attacks, by the author of *The Killing Fields*.

The Village in the Jungle by Leonard

Woolf. Hogarth, London, 1961 (orig. pub. 1913). The famous novel of Ceylonese village life by the husband of Virginia Woolf. Leonard Woolf served in the Ceylon Civil Service for seven years.

Pictorial

Ceylon by Lionel Wendt. Lincolns-Prayer, 1950. Lionel Wendt was perhaps the first photographer to look at Ceylon without the blinkers of a Colonial sensibility. Not an easy book to get hold of, unfortunately.

Island Ceylon designed and photographed by Roloff Beny. Thames & Hudson, London, 1970. Fine photography and subject selection. Text by John Lindsay Opie includes an edited anthology of writing on the island and its history.

Sri Lanka: Island Civilisation by Senaka Bandaranayake, photography by Christian and Nadine Zuber. Lake House, Colombo, 1978. Overview of the island and its people, written by noted archaeologist and historian.

Sri Lanka by Tim Page. Lake House, Colombo, 1985. Views of the island by a famous photographer. Text by Nigel Palmer.

The Book of Ceylon by H W Cave, with photographs by the author. Cassell, London, 1908. Written in contemporary guidebook style, the book's chief attraction lies in the multitude of photographs of turn-of-the-century Ceylon with which it is illustrated.

The Wild, the Free, the Beautiful by Nihal Fernando. Studio Times, Colombo, 1987. Studies of Sri Lanka — landscapes, wildlife and people — by one of the finest and most unaffected Sri Lankan photographers.

Others

Drawings from the Royal Botanical Gardens, Peradeniya by Laki Senanayake. Norprint, Colombo,

1982. Folio edition of botanical portraits by a famous Sri Lankan artist.

Recollections of Ceylon after a Residence of Nearly Thirteen Years by The Rev. James Selkirk. J Hatchard & Son, London, 1844. Personal memoir, general observations and translation into English of the *Prataya Sataka*. Interesting and often amusing for its exemplification of Colonial attitudes towards the people and the country.

SELECTED FILMOGRAPHY
(courtesy Manik Sandrasagara and Transervice Limited)

The following is a short list of documentary films on Sri Lanka. It is by no means exhaustive, but intended only to indicate the range of available material. No feature films have been included; there is a dearth of good English-language material, and films in Sinhala will be of little interest to those who cannot understand the language.

General

A Gem Called Sri Lanka. Ceylon Tourist Board, 23 min. A promotional film emphasising arts, crafts and festivals.

Destination Sri Lanka dir. John Burder. Ceylon Tourist Board, 31 min. A promotional film aimed at travel agents, covering available facilities and tourist attractions.

Dream of Kings dir. Tissa Abeysekera. Mahaveli Authority of Sri Lanka/Worldview International Foundation. 28 min. Documentary on the Mahaveli Project, dealing with five separate sub-schemes within the main project.

Forty Leagues from Paradise dir. Lester James Pieris. Ceylon Tourist Board, 20 min. Impressions of the country by Sri Lanka's greatest film director.

Hill Capital dir. Guilo Petroni. 1950, Government Film Unit, 24 min. This black-and-white production is a look at Kandy, its past and its arts, by a former Director of the Government Film Unit.

Temples, Tea and a Thousand Festivals dir. Walter Kneise. Ceylon Tourist Board, 30 min. Promotional documentary.

History & Culture

Heritage of Lanka dir. Ralph Keene. 1952, Government Film Unit, 20 min. Black-and-white documentary on four of the country's most-visited ancient sites: Anuradhapura, Mihintale, Polonnaruwa and Sri Pada (Adam's Peak).

Jetavana Monastery Conservation Project dir. Ashley de Vos. 30 min. Documentary on the efforts to restore Jetavana Monastery, part of the 'Cultural Triangle' project.

Rajarata, Land of Kings dir. Keith Wood. Ceylon Tourist Board. The Rajarata was the land of the ancient capitals: Anuradhapura, Dambulla, Polonnaruwa and Sigiriya. Film discusses all four sites, part of the cultural heritage of modern Sri Lanka.

Sri Lanka the Resplendent dir. Francine Vande-Wiele. UNESCO, 25 min. Said to be one of finest contemporary documentaries, depicts domestic culture and traditions in relation to the preservation of ancient sites in the Rajarata.

Beneath the Seas of Ceylon dir. Mike Wilson. 1957, Ceylon Tourist Board, 20 min. First underwater documentary made in Sri Lanka. Sequence showing taming of giant groupers by Rodney Jonklaas is a standout.

Ruhunu National Park. 1952, Ceylon Tourist Board, 14 min. Period footage of a trip through Ruhunu National Park, or Yala, as it is better known.

Sri Lanka Sanctuary. Ceylon Tourist Board, 10 min. Film on Yala and Wilpattu sanctuaries.

Agriculture

World of Tea. UNICEF/Worldview International Foundation, 30 min. Examines economic and social problems inherent in Sri Lanka tea industry, and efforts being made to solve them.

Society & Culture

Dance of Siva dir. Chidananda Das Gupta and B D Garga. United States Information Service, 40 min. A tribute to the great art historian and defender of traditional culture. Original score by Ravi Shankar.

Fishermen of Negombo dir. George Wickremesinghe. 1952, Government Film Unit, 19 min. Lyrical black-and-white documentary on Sri Lanka's largest fishing community, made at a time when fishing techniques and equipment were still very traditional.

Meditation dir. Paul Zils. Government Film Unit, 20 min. Documentary about a doctor who renounces the world in the middle of life to put on a *bikkhu*'s robes.

Dance & Drama

Songs and Drums of Sri Lanka dir. Deben Battacharya. Ceylon Tourist Board, 25 min. Traditional Sri Lankan ritual and ceremony captured in a village environment.

Festivals

Festival of the August Moon dir. Lester James Pieris. Ceylon Tourist Board, 25 min. Fine documentary on the Kandy Perahera by the great film director.

GLOSSARY

All words are Sinhalese unless otherwise denoted. Sinh. = Sinhalese, Tam. = Tamil, Eng. =English, Skt. = Sanskrit, Port. = Portuguese. In many cases, the word may be the same in Sinhala, Tamil and/or Pali and Sanskrit.

Words in CAPITALS within the body of any reference have their own separate Glossary references.

SOURCES

A Dictionary of the Sinhalese Language, Wilhelm Geiger *et al*, Royal Asiatic Society (Ceylon Branch), Colombo, 1935

A Sinhalese–English Dictionary, Charles Carter, pub Baptist Missionary Society, cprt M D Gunasena & Co Ltd, Colombo

A Sanskrit–English Dictionary, Sir Monier Monier-Williams *et al*, Clarendon Press, Oxford, 1960

A Portuguese and English Pronouncing Dictionary, Joao Fernandes Valdez, Livraria Garnier, Rio de Janeiro and Paris

Ambalama
a rest-house or roadside shelter for travellers.

Ambarella
hog-plum, a rather tart-tasting fruit like a small mango; tree bearing the fruit, *Spondias mangifera*.

Arahat
a Buddhist 'saint'; more accurately, one who is wholly pure of mind and therefore sanctified.

Arathi
(Tam.) a ceremony in which a lamp or other significant object is waved before a person or the image of a deity to be honoured.

Asura, Asuraya
a kind of demon or Titan in Hindu (and therefore Buddhist) mythology. Rebelling against the gods, they were put down by Skanda (Kartikeya or Kataragama Deviyo), and now live at the foot of Mount Meru. (See index and text.)

Avurudda
(pl. and adj. *Avurudu*) a year; specifically, the Sinhalese New Year (Aluth Avurudda).

Ayubovan
traditional Sinhalese greeting and farewell, accompanied by hands clasped in front of the face. The word means 'may your age increase', i.e. may you live long.

Ayurveda
(Skt.) study of health and medicine, one of the ancient 'sacred sciences'. (Sinh.) Only used in reference to the traditional (as opposed to Western) system of medicine.

Bervaya
(pl. *Beravayo*) a man of the Drummer caste.

Bhagavad Gita
(Skt., lit. 'Krishna's Song') mystical poem that forms part of the MAHA-BHARATA and takes the form of a dialogue between Krishna and Arjuna. It contains many of the principal ideas of Vedantic Hinduism.

Bikkhu
a Buddhist 'monk'. See SANGHA.

Bo
peepul or sacred fig tree, *Ficus religiosa*. The Buddha is said to have attained Enlightenment while meditating beneath such a tree.

Cadjan
(Eng. fm. Malay *kajang*) Anglo-Indian word for thatching made of plaited coconut-palm fronds.

Chena
(fm. Sinh. *hena*) dry land, usually forest clearing, cultivated at intervals of several years.

Conquista Espiritual
(Port. 'spiritual conquest') the conversion of the native peoples of the East to Roman Catholicism by Portuguese missionaries.

Culavamsa
See MAHAVAMSA.

Dagoba
a stupa; a dome-shaped building, often of colossal size, housing a relic or relics of the Buddha.

Dalada
the Sacred Tooth, a relic of the Buddha; Sri Lanka's greatest national treasure.

Dalada Maligawa
the Temple of the Tooth by the lakeside at Kandy, where the Sacred Tooth resides.

Dhammachakra, Dhammacakka
building erected in Anuradhapura by King Devanampiyatissa and used by King Sri Meghavanna to house the Sacred Tooth.

Dana, Danaya
alms or a gift of any sort; (colloq.) an alms-giving.

Dansala, Dana Salava
an alms-hall.

Devale, Devalaya
a shrine or temple to a Hindu god, usually one where Buddhists also worship. (See index and text.)

Dhamma (Skt. **Dharma**)
1. law or doctrine. 2. the principles of justice and virtue. 3. the teachings of the Buddha as preserved in the scriptures. The third is the commonest application of the word and incorporates the other two meanings.

Esala
1. the lunar month July–August. 2. senna, a medicinal and ornamental tree, *Cassia fistula*. In recent times it has been replaced in the KAP ceremony that precedes the Kandy PERAHERA by a young JAK tree.

Gama
(adj. and pl. *Gam*) village or hamlet.

Gaman Hewisi
marching drums; the Sinhalese war-march.

Ganu-denu
barter, traffic or transaction; an exchange. Specifically the traditional exchange of money in the AVURUDU ceremonies.

Gokkola
frond of the coconut palm. Young palm-fronds are used to make intricate decorations for weddings and other festive occasions.

A popular representation of Visnu with good words on the hands.

Nadagama

(adj. and pl. *Nadagam*) drama involving prose and verse, dance and group singing, derived from Catholic liturgical drama but was expanded to include historical, mythological and contemporary subjects.

Naga

semi-divine beings, half human and half serpent and capable of assuming either form. Nagas were said to have inhabited Lanka, with the YAKKHAS, before the coming of Man.

Nekatha

1. star, planet or other astrological element; hence, 2. the astrologically-determined auspicious moment for commencing any act or enterprise.

Nonagatha

1. an inauspicious time for the commencement of an act or enterprise. 2. time between the end of the old year and the beginning of the new, also deemed to be highly inauspicious.

Parangiya

1. man of Portugal. (adj. & pl. *Parangi*) 2. syphilis.

Paslo, Panchaloha

lit. 'five metals'; alloy of gold, silver, copper, iron and lead, or copper, lead, tin and iron, used by jewellers.

Peepul

See Bo.

Perahera

a pageant or procession, usually of a religious nature. The Esala Perahera in Kandy is the best known.

Poruwa

1. a board or plank. 2. the dais on which bride and groom sit during the Sinhalese marriage ceremony.

Puja, Pooja

oblation or sacrifice.

Rajakariya

'king's work' 1. compulsory public service owed by all landowners to the crown. 2. public duty or office.

Ramayana

'Romance of Rama', Indian epic of prob. post 3rd cent. BC. Recounts the story of Prince Rama: childhood, marriage to Princess Sita, her abduction by the evil King Ravana, and their reunion after a great battle in which Rama defeats King Ravana. Ravana's kingdom is identified with the island of Lanka.

Randoli

a golden palanquin, the conveyance of a queen or a goddess.

Rodiya

man of the lowest Sinhalese caste. The Rodiyas' low status was due to their hereditary occupation as tanners, makers of hide ropes and handlers of animal carcasses.

Sakyamuni

'Sage of the Sakyas'; name applied to Gautama Buddha, who was a prince of the Sakya clan.

Sal, Sala

resinous tree, *Vateria acuminata.*

Samsara

lit. 'wandering'. The travels of the self through the cycle of birth and rebirth, an unhappy condition from which it must be liberated.

Sangha

the brotherhood of BIKKHUS, those who have renounced the world of the senses to live according to the principles set forth by the Buddha.

Sari, Saree

(Eng. fm. Hindi *sari*) a woman's garment consisting of a single sheet of silk or fine cloth, usually about six yards long, wrapped and artfully draped about the body.

Sarong

(Eng. fm. Malay *sarong*) usually a man's garment, rather like a skirt, folded over and tied about the waist.

Senapati, Senadhipati

general or commander-in-chief of an army.

Sil

1. morality. 2. a set of moral strictures, ten in all, of which five are to be followed by all Buddhists at all times, three more by laymen on certain occasions ('taking sil') and all ten by monks and nuns.

Talpat, Talapat

palmyrah palm, *Borassus flabelliformis*; the leaves are used for writing on.

Tesavalamai, Thesawalamai

(Tam.) system of laws applicable only to the Tamils of Jaffna. Originally a system of customary laws connected with the Tamil system of matrilineage, it underwent many modifications before being codified by the Dutch around 1707.

Thovil, Thovila

ritual exorcism.

Vedas

(Skt. *veda*, knowledge, usually true or sacred knowledge). Hindu religious works of great antiquity (the oldest, the *Rigveda*, is said to date to around 4000 BC), containing many of the fundamental principles of Hindu philosophy.

Vellala, Vellalar

(Tam.) man of the Farmer caste. As with the GOVIGAMA, the Vellala are held to be the highest caste among Sri Lankan Tamils.

Ves

1. a mask or disguise 2. a special headdress awarded to a Kandyan dancer on completion of his apprenticeship.

Vihare

a Buddhist 'monastery'.

Wood-apple

(Sinh. *beli*) Bengal quince, a hard-shelled fruit with a brown, pulpy heart and characteristic odour; the tree is *Feronia elephantum.*

Yakdessa

a shaman; director of the Kohomba Kankariya ritual, the highest development of the Kandyan dance.

Yakkha, Yakka

demon or nature-spirit; along with NAGAS, the original inhabitants of Lanka in prehistoric times.

Yakkini, Yakkhini

fem. of YAKKHA.

Yala

secondary paddy growing season, October to February. See MAHA.

Goviya
(adj. *Govi*) a farmer, specifically a paddy-farmer.

Govigama
the Farmer caste, held to be the highest caste among the Sinhalese.

Horaneva
a curved ceremonial horn or bugle.

Jak
(Eng. fm. Malayalam *chakka*) a large fruit resembling breadfruit in taste and texture; also the tree that bears it, *Artocarpus integrifolia.*

Jambu
rose-apple, a small, pink, bell-shaped fruit; also the tree of same name, *Eugenia jambos.*

Jataka
birth; specifically the 'birth-stories' of the Buddha, accounts of his 550 previous incarnations as a Bodhisattva or entelechic Buddha, recounted by the Master himself.

Kap
a vow, usually to the goddess Pattini, that a certain ceremony will be held. It takes the form of planting a stake made from a freshly-felled tree with appropriate ritual at the site of the ceremony. Kap is planted before the Kandy Perahera and the Kataragama Festival.

Karma
(Sinh. & Skt.) 1. act or deed. 2. the merit or demerit acquired by the individual as a result of (1), which will affect his life and lives to come in a deterministic way. 3. the principle of 'action and reaction' by which these consequences are effected. Often confused with the Western concept of Destiny, it is in fact quite a different thing, since predestination is not involved.

Kattadiya
a 'devil-priest' or shaman; the presiding figure at a Southern Thovil.

Kocchi
a very small, very hot chilli, white in colour.

Kolam, Kolama
Sinhalese folk theatre, a combination of masked dance and drama. The plots are traditional.

Kovil
(Tam.) a Hindu temple.

Koviyar
(Tam.) originally, highest of three classes of slaves owned by the Vellala, or landowning, caste. Though no longer bound, they still perform various ceremonial services for the Vellala on such occasions as weddings, comings-of-age and the like.

Kurakkan
a sort of millet, *Elusine coracana,* used to make *stringhoppers, pittu* and sweetmeats.

Lovi-lovi
a small cherry-red fruit, *Flacourtia inermis,* extremely sour.

Magul Kapuwa
1. (archaic) royal barber or valet.
2. professional matchmaker.

Maha
1. large or great, as in Mahavamsa.
2. principal paddy growing season, March to September.

Mahabharata
(Skt.) 'The Great Epic of the Bharatas', ancient Indian epic poem probably based on actual events occurring between 1400 and 1000 BC, concerning a power struggle between two related families, the Pandavas and the Kauravas. Incorporates the Bhagavad Gita.

Mahavamsa
'Great Chronicle', historical chronicle of Sri Lanka dealing chiefly with the history of Buddhism on the island and with the royal succession. It covers events from Vijayan (6th cent. BC) times to the early 4th cent. AD, and includes accounts of the apocryphal visits to the island by the Buddha in prehistoric times. **Culavamsa**, the 'Lesser Chronicle', continues the account up to Colonial times.

Malabar
(Eng., adj.) of or from the Malabar Coast, which is the southwestern seaboard of India, from Goa down to the tip of the subcontinent, bounded by the Western Ghats to the east and incorporating the states of Kerala and Karnatka.

Maname Jataka, Maname Katawa
one of the Jakatas. Prince Maname and his new bride are returning home through a forest when they encounter a band of hunters. An argument breaks out, and in the ensuing battle Maname vanquishes the entire band before challenging the hunter-king to a duel. Meanwhile, the princess has fallen in love with the hunter-king, and through her treachery, Maname is killed. Despite her pleas, the hunter-king then strips the princess of her jewellery and leaves her in the forest, observing that if she was so ready to betray her lawful husband, she would probably do the same to him.

Mangosteen
(Eng. fm. Malay *mangustan*) reddish-brown fruit with a hard outer shell and 6–8 sweet, white inner segments; tree bearing such fruit, *Garcina mangostana.*

Maya
(Skt.) 1. trick, deception or illusion.
2. the illusion that is the source of the perceptual Universe. (This word has several other meanings.)

Mudaliyar, Mudiyanse
a Kandyan hereditary title; the chief revenue officer of a district.

Mudra
(Skt.) 1. a seal or stamp. 2. an instrument for sealing or stamping. 3. one of 24 positions of the hand and fingers, every one of which has a particular esoteric or mystical significance.

Must
(Anglo-Indian) annual condition affecting adult male elephants. Symptoms include a swelling and secretion from the temporal gland located behind the eye, and behavioural changes that render it intractable and unpredictable.

ACKNOWLEDGMENTS

A year has passed since this book was completed in manuscript, and it has been an eventful one for Sri Lanka. The authors wish to dedicate this book to their families and to all those whose belief in the future remains untarnished in spite of those events and who, in diverse ways, are working to restore the peace and felicity the people of Sri Lanka once regarded as their birthright.

The authors would like to thank the Director of the Ambalangoda Mask Museum for giving them access to his collection of masks, Mr A P Fonseka of Plate & Co. for permission to use their archival pictures, Koshika Sandrasagara for permission to use her painting of L T P Manjusri, and the Secretary General of Parliament, Mr S N Senaviratne, for permission to photograph Parliament in session. Special thanks also go out to the following people without whose help this book could not have been published: Chelvadurai Anjelendran, Tilak Conrad, Christo de Alwis, Aruni Dewaraja, Lorna Dewaraja, Richard de Zoysa, R M Ekernayake, Nihal Fernando who has been a great source of inspiration, Lucinda Hartley, Swami Siva Kalki, Velayuthapillai Kunathungan, Ronald Lewcock, Kushan Manjusri, Mrs L T P Manjusri, Feizal Mansoor, Luxshman Nadaraja, Kumar Pereira, Mahesh Perera, Marius Perera, Ismeth Raheem, Asoka Ratwatte, Manik Sandrasagara, Barbara Sansoni, Peter Schoppert, Laki Senanayake, Shirley Soh, everybody at Thompson Lanka, and Gamini Wijetunge.